GOD
IS A
SALESMAN

GOD
IS A
SALESMAN
LEARN FROM THE MASTER

MARK STEVENS

CENTER
STREET®
New York Boston Nashville

Center Street
Hachette Book Group USA
237 Park Avenue
New York, NY 10017

Visit our Web site at www.centerstreet.com.

Center Street is a division of Hachette Book Group USA, Inc. The Center Street name and logo is a trademark of Hachette Book Group USA, Inc.

Printed in the United States of America

First Edition: January 2008
10 9 8 7 6 5 4 3 2 1

Library of Congress Cataloging-in-Publication Data
Stevens, Mark, 1947-
    God is a salesman : learn from the master / Mark Stevens.
        p. cm.
    ISBN-13: 978-1-59995-690-9
    ISBN-10: 1-59995-690-X
  1. Selling. 2. Customer relations. 3. Consumer satisfaction. 4. Success in business.
  I. Title.

    HF5438.25.S7376 2007
    658.85—dc22   2007005915

Book design by Charles Sutherland

One overpowering trait distinguishes exceptional people from the masses who live and die without making their mark in the world . . . without accomplishing significant achievements. That trait is the drive to learn, to grow, to identify new and more effective ways of engaging in their personal and business endeavors. Those who are determined to escape the bounds of gravity will find that God has created a profound blueprint for success. This book will help you to identify it . . . and use it to greatly enrich your life.

Jesus said to him, "Thomas, because you have seen Me, you have believed. Blessed are those who have not seen and yet have believed."

John 20:29 (NKJV)

CONTENTS

GOD
IS A
SALESMAN

INTRODUCTION

Genesis

Modern man is inclined to disbelieve. To be skeptical. To need evidence of what he is asked to trust and have faith in.

At the same time, billions of modern men and women abandon this disbelief and this skepticism when it comes to one thing: embracing God.

Why this paradox? How can it be? In an increasingly scientific and empirical world—where people are drawn more to information technology than poetry, where the science of genetics is viewed as more powerful in shaping human behavior than parental influence—what accounts for the unprecedented worship of a spirit we cannot see, touch, examine, or observe in a scientific setting? Of a god?

Interestingly, at time of great conflict and dissension across the globe and among varying cultures, the one universal constant that drives human thought and actions is belief and faith in God. This can be explained in only one way: God, or specifically the religions that celebrate and explain Him, is a salesman. The world's master salesman.

I say this with awe and utmost respect. With the knowledge that it is vital for us to have faith in a Force without the ability to shake His hand or scientifically prove His existence. He will not tolerate this kind of investigation. We believe because we believe. And God prompts this belief through a profound set of principles that, if we understand them and why they prompt our faith in Him, will help us to achieve greater success and depth in our personal lives. Our careers. And our businesses. God is a salesman . . . we can learn from The Master. And this is a good and powerful fact of life.

God Is a Salesman is about success. How to achieve it as a *salesperson*, a business person, a parent, or a spouse by understanding God, religion, spirituality, and faith from a new perspective. By viewing the power of God through a prism and seeing how it can apply to, and vastly improve, those aspects of your life that you may not now associate with God.

Perpetual Discovery

God Is a Salesman is more than a set of rules or observations. It is based on, and reflects, a way of life. I did not gather the key principles from textbooks or interviews. I discovered them through personal epiphanies. Through the deep thought, spirituality, and philosophy that form the basic tenets of my life. In my restless and constant pursuit of God and how faith in Him can add richness to my life and my loved ones, I engage in perpetual discovery. Not by simply marching into a house of worship, dutifully reading what others have written, and then going back to business as usual. Instead, I have been, and remain, determined to discover for myself. And thus the insights and spiritual framework built into *God Is a Salesman* are the product of one man's communion with God. Through deep thought, hikes through the wilderness, and constant introspection, I have been committed to gain a special kind of knowledge and determined to know how and why this can be applied to everyday life. To family. To business. To salesmanship.

If we understand how and why we have faith in God, we can use this power to create and lead more successful lives. Yes, as salespeople if that is your professional endeavor, but also in every other role you may play: doctor, lawyer, mother, father, senior executive, and junior manager. Those who take pride in being salespeople, and others who shudder at the very idea, have more in common than they realize. In many aspects of all of our lives, we are *salespeople*. So the question we must ask is: How well (or how poorly) can we perform in this critical role? And how can we raise the bar?

The Master has much to teach us. All we have to do is open our eyes and minds to His lessons. Come with me. You will find them to be extraordinary.

A Greater Truth

You have never seen Him. You do not know if *He* is a *Him*. He has never said a word to you. Never shown His face. Never revealed if He is Caucasian, Black, Asian, or Latin.

You don't know how old He is. Or if *age* applies to Him at all. You don't know if He was *born* or just *appeared*. Or if He is a *being* or a *spirit* or both.

You know of Him only from the Bible and other holy texts. You have no tangible evidence that He exists. And yet you, and billions like you, believe in Him. To one degree or another, admitted, or hidden away in the recesses of our minds, we worship and pray to Him.

He is God.

Without a scintilla of the proof we demand of everything else, we embrace Him as fact. No *60 MINUTES* investigations. No FBI interrogations. Yes, a glimmer of doubt slips in the back door of our minds now and then, but we are loath to give in to it and it passes just as quickly as it arrives.

Why? Because God is a *salesman*. More than that. He actually is the greatest *salesman* of all time. And this is a blessing.

4

Why do I say God is a salesman and that this is a blessing? Because billions of men, women, and children worship a god. We gather in churches, temples, synagogues, and mosques, and we are comforted by our God's *presence*. It adds a rich dimension to our lives. His aura is the wellspring of our faith, courage, and belief in more than the bric-a-brac of daily existence. And this belief brings a deeper meaning to life than what we are capable of identifying with the naked eye.

Think of it this way. Life throws curve balls at you. You can't stop them from coming and you can't just duck. You have to deal with them and how well you do is the acid test of a life just lived or a life lived with faith. The difference is monumental. The former is just going through the motions, filling space from cradle to grave. The latter is a rich and exhilarating experience.

Consider a curve ball I experienced out of the blue. My wife of thirty-one years, Carol Ann Stevens, and I had just returned from a magical vacation in the Caribbean. It was January, 2006, and we had traded a week of winter chill for the warm caress of balmy trade winds, blue skies, and azure water. On vacation, I was feeling like the exceptionally healthy physical specimen I appeared to be: slim, athletic, a daily jogger, and devoted hiker. On the surface, I was a poster boy for middle-aged fitness. And then in one of those chain-reaction nightmares, I was whisked from the beach alongside San Juan's Ritz-Carlton Hotel, flown to New York, and rushed by ambulance to Manhattan's New York-Presbyterian Hospital for quadruple by-pass surgery by world-famed cardiothoracic surgeon Craig Smith (who had applied his skill to former President Bill Clinton a year before).

"How can this be happening?" I wondered.

The doctors explained that I was a classic victim of anemic cardiovascular genes, the son of a man who had died of heart disease at age forty. Specifically, I was plagued by a time bomb called *silent ischemia*. From all outward appearances, I looked like a fit specimen, but I was actually a jog away from a massive heart attack. In an instant, I had to face the truth that I needed massive heart surgery, and it hit me with a vengeance. I would face an eight-hour procedure carrying a risk of stroke, long-term disability, and death. In one fell swoop, the life I adored—round-the-clock working, running, dining out, watching movies—appeared to be vanishing before my eyes.

For an hour, I was crestfallen, morose, feeling terribly sorry for myself. Concerned about my family and my business. I worried that even if the surgery was successful, I would age overnight and be a shadow of my former self. Alone in my ninth-floor hospital room overlooking the Hudson River, awaiting my wife who was being paged from the visitor's room, I played a tragic movie in my mind. The story line had a black beginning and an even bleaker end: Mark Stevens' life, as I knew it, was over.

When I heard my wife's familiar footsteps approaching my room, I cried. When my sons arrived an hour later, I cried again. I worried that I might soon be deprived of seeing their beautiful faces, of their friendship, of the grasp of their hands. And then just as I was about to wail about how terrible this all was, the sadness suddenly lifted and floated away just as a fog lifts under the brilliance of an August sun. Instantly, and somehow magically, I found myself in a cocoon of calm, courage, and peace all at the same time; I didn't think of why the change occurred. I just knew it did, and that it was a great relief.

My surgery was scheduled for the following week, which meant I had to remain in the hospital, in a virtual holding pattern, letting the clock tick until the Plavix administered to me as an emergency precaution left my body and my platelets reconstituted themselves. But the wait never wore on me for a moment. The hospital stay was actually a joy. Friends and family visiting, meeting new people, experiencing the warmth of the really special nurses, the Florence Nightingales, who demonstrated true humanity and genuine care. Even as I was rolled down to the operating room on D-Day (without an ounce of sedation), I was serene.

When the nurse asked me for my favorite psalm, I

answered the twenty-third and she cited it from memory. I loved the words—always did ("the Lord is my shepherd . . .")—but I did not need them for comfort. I was already at peace.

What accounted for this extraordinary calm? Was it really magical? I don't think so. I now believe it was my faith. I recognized instinctively that my fate was out of my hands and in God's. And I also understood at that very time of crisis that my surgery, whether it took me out the hospital's back door in a casket or through the front door to my family, would all be part of the wonderful voyage God has blessed me with.

A few days before the surgery, I gathered Carol and my sons, Harly and Justin, around me, and shared with them what was in my heart and why I was at peace.

"I know you want me to be optimistic and to see this surgery as routine as a blood test, but my wife, my sons, I am having **open heart surgery.** I will be in the operating room for more than eight hours. And the surgeons will be operating on my cardiovascular system, not my legs or my back, and in this theatre, anything can happen. Although this is a wonderful hospital and Dr. Smith is world-class, I will be going through heavy-duty surgery and my life will be at risk."

Before Carol and the boys could squeeze in reassuring words, I continued: "The risk is not the most important thing. Most important is that I have already had an amazing life. The gift God has given me is extraordinary and joyous. So if I die, I know you will miss me and be sad. But please let it comfort you that my life will not be cut short. It has already been the equivalent of an infinite journey, and although I would love to have more time with you and the trees and the skies, I am content and at peace whatever the outcome because I have had a complete life."

As I lay in the hospital bed, my family gathered around me, I was driven by faith, not fear. There were no visions of angels. No trumpets heralding pearly gates. Nothing specific and yet everything highly specific. In place of the initial tearjerker film, a happy movie filled my mind, the kind made possible only by a richly rewarding and highly-successful life. And by a profound sense of faith.

In the context of this book, a *salesman* is not a huckster. Not a Willy Loman. Not a Xerox rep with a quota to fill. Not a *salesman* as many of us use the term in everyday life.

When I say God is a *salesman*, I mean an influencer, an educator, and a force that enables us to bridge the gap between what we see and what may well be the greater truth. And this extraordinary capability can be critical to all of us in our various roles. Clearly, we are not gods. Not by a long shot. But if we delve into the dynamics that underlie our faith in God, in religion, we can acquire even more powerful skills as human beings.

Let's step back for a moment. The word *salesmanship* has come to signify a quality that is crude, manipulative, crass, and bogus. But this is a distorted way of viewing a critically important skill. Assume you are a parent. From the earliest days of their lives, you want to steer your children toward appropriate ways of behavior by teaching them honor, responsibility, respect, drive, determination, and commitment. They do not emerge from the womb with a natural inclination to *play well with others*. You have to *sell* them on that. They may have a winning spirit embedded in their DNA, but when they see their friends playing Frisbee on a warm spring day, they will want to abandon their homework and rush off to join the game. You have to *sell* them on the advantage of staying glued to their books until the assignment is done. And done right.

Your guidance of the child's behavior springs from a reservoir of experience you have gained over the years. You have witnessed the success that has come to others—perhaps yourself included—who have made the sacrifice to achieve their goals and, conversely, the fate of others who have failed to do so.

A similar scenario unfolds with many salespeople, often young ones, who lack the benefit of perspective. They view each prospect as a potential transaction ("let me sell them something now") instead of seeing the far more valuable and rewarding achievement of building a relationship over time. As a mentor and guide, my role is to teach them the wisdom of slowing down—not speeding up—of having the discipline to grow something genuine and enduring.

There are times when perspective advises that you take the opposite course. Assume you believe the time has come for your employer to reward your excellent performance with a raise. Yes, exemplary performance on the job should automatically be greeted with a more generous paycheck and an elevated title, but life rarely comes wrapped in such presents-under-the-tree-Christmas-morning packages. Those who sit in silent expectation . . . and wait, wait, wait . . . seldom receive their due rewards. To get what you deserve, you have to *sell* yourself.

Success in life and the ability to *sell* are inexorably bound. Whether you are moving Chevies off a showroom floor, inspiring others to achieve a goal, or spreading your philosophy on how best to engage in real estate investing, you have to *sell*. You have to educate. You have to influence.

Which brings us back to God. Specifically, how we can learn from The Master.

Respect for God should not hinder us from understanding the way religion leads, inspires, motivates, and educates us to have faith in God, and based on this to improve ourselves. Not as gods. But as mortals searching for the most productive, successful, and enjoyable careers and lives. Who else should we turn to as role models: motivational speakers? College professors? Hollywood celebrities? Sales trainers? Ridiculous. We are far wiser to look to God. To the source of The Greater Truth.

The best salespeople never look like they are selling anything. And technically, they are not. They are educating, instilling faith and confidence. They are quietly and invisibly demonstrating why you should believe in them and, in turn, *buy* from them. A lesson we can learn from religion.

Think of it this way: God never sells vacuum cleaners, shoes, or productivity software. And neither should you. Even if you are a vacuum cleaner, shoe, or productivity software salesperson, you need to learn from The Master. And The Master sells one thing: ideas. So there you are slinging product samples over your back, selling (or on any given day, trying to sell) products—but the world wants ideas. How do you sell vacuum cleaners as *ideas?* How about on the basis of providing for a clean and attractive home? Of course, this is not the only way to sell vacuum cleaners, but the principle is inviolate: No one wants to buy noisy machines with belts and fans and suction devices. Do you ever wake up dreaming of that? Of course not. But we do want to have clean and comfortable homes, and that's what the best vacuum cleaner salespeople will sell.

What are you selling? Paradoxically, what you don't *sell* is likely more powerful and important than what you *sell*.

Recently, I was strolling along a charming piazza in Venice when I spotted a watch store. I had no need for a new watch. A fine Cartier graced my wrist and three more watches were in my dresser at home. But the alure of the shop—quaint, stylish, old-world Italian —drew me in and within moments I was transported to nineteenth-century Italy and the genesis of an elegant jewelry business that would evolve into the world-renowned Bulgari brand.

A master raconteur, who happened to be the shop's owner, led my voyage through the time passages. With extraordinary grace, he wove the story of the Bulgaris and their meticulous attention to design. Before I knew it, a smashing jewel of a watch was strapped to my wrist as the story of the family's artistic vision continued with compelling and beguiling detail. Soon after, I was strolling the piazza again, the beaming owner of a $5,000 timepiece I did not need, but now adored.

I tell this story because it reveals an important business lesson. We all have to serve as salespeople in one form or another. And when you do, remember the story of my Italian time traveler: The best salespeople are invisible. They never look like they are selling anything.

You can write off this storyteller as a gifted merchant, which he may be (although it's unlikely, given his shoebox of a shop; Sam Walton—the king of thinking big—would have thought so), but I believe he is driven more by a passion for ideas rather than for sales. Interestingly, armed with that passion, the sale is a near certainty.

Let's think about what Jesus did with His life: He sowed ideas. He didn't look like He was *selling* because He wasn't. While the multitudes around Him were accepting life as it was, Jesus was advocating for a better way, a kinder way, a more meaningful way. Was Jesus a *salesman*? Today, 2007 years after His crucifixion, there are two billion Christians roaming the planet and the faithful are growing. If Jesus and the religion He fostered did not *sell* faith majestically and invisibly, those two billion human souls would be adrift from what for many is the most important anchor in their lives.

Consider the power of it all: God, or the religions that

explain and celebrate Him, prompt us to believe that He:

- Exists.
- Created the world.
- Is all goodness.
- Is all knowing.
- Loves us.

Without a shard of proof or a scintilla of traditional CSI-type evidence that all of this is true, we embrace Him, adore Him, and worship Him. What force is responsible for this phenomenon? What characteristics can we derive from our faith in God that can teach all of us how to educate, influence, and *sell* more effectively? How does The Master do it? What can we learn from Him? From the ways religions build and maintain their power base? Their congregations?

Examine the key principles behind this power and this phenomenon. Not for the sake of religious discovery alone, but also to identify the techniques God and religion utilize so that we, in turn, can employ these dynamics in our lives. Let's explore them one at a time.

1

God Treats Us All as Family

Belief in God, the scriptures advise us, assures us of the following:

- We are loved by our Creator.
- Nothing we do can diminish that love.
- God will be with us for all of our lives.
- God is omnipotent, omnipresent, all knowing, and all powerful.

What does this have to do with salesmanship? Let's explore what the traditional view of selling is all about. Typically, people who sell view it as a way to manipulate others. To get them to buy things from you. To score, as if in a contest.

You know the drill all too well (as do your prospects): A salesperson develops a pitch, targets and woos the mark; if all goes well, the mark takes the bait, the sales-person celebrates and moves on to the next mark. This is a crude view of the process, perhaps, but painfully close to the way the cheese-in-the-mousetrap scenario is supposed to unfold according to the gospel of classic *salesmanship*. The question is: Does this represent a genuine relation-ship between the seller and the buyer? No way! Save for a few precious exceptions, it amounts to *us vs. them* com-bat—slick, superficial, plastic, and often based on a form of deception. The salesperson pretends to care about the prospect/customer but, in fact, only cares about bagging his prey. The better the salesperson, the less transparent this is, but it still IS!

The time has come to rethink the entire process.

To do so, we have to dial back for a moment. We must view *selling* as a way of *building and maintaining faith in one another*. That is more than semantics; it is a novel phi-losophy. And as surprising as it may be, developing and incorporating a new philosophy is a key component of the transition from selling in the standard Willy Loman manner to *selling* in a format that resembles and learns from The Master.

Our philosophy begins with the recognition that we are all God's children. We have faith in Him because we are members of the family of God. Think of how impor-tant and powerful this is: If we are doubters, God doesn't treat us as prospects or, if we are believers, as customers. Instead, we are all members of the family of God, believers and disbelievers alike.

Everyone who *sells* anything must pause and reflect on this, not for its religious significance (although it is based on religious roots) but because it has profound and pragmatic implications for the world of business. The wise salesperson will learn from The Master and relate to customers and prospects as virtual family members as opposed to strangers, targets, or marks to be sold!

Traditional selling is infused with a mythology, a Holy Grail of sorts, that is pure nonsense. Worse than that, it is a route to mediocrity at best, and more likely a route to failure.

It is time to reinvent the traditional view of selling. Now!

Think of the conventional wisdom about selling as The Myths of Willy Loman:

Myth: A good salesperson has the gift of gab.

Reality: Gab? Does anyone want gab? How fast do you run from that? A good salesperson acquires the gift of identifying what customers and prospects really want and finds a way to satisfy that. His talk is not of gab, but of substance and demonstrable value.

Myth: The salesperson is the hunter and the prospect is the prey.

Reality: What a shortsighted way to view the process of building and nurturing lifelong relationships. A hunt or a battle? That's not selling: It is war and great salespeople never, ever want to engage in war with their customers. Those who do may make their quotas, but they will never earn the trust, respect, and loyalty that drives exceptional relationships and, in turn, extraordinary careers. The real winners align themselves with their customers as opposed to pitting themselves against them.

Myth: Selling is just another component of the business process.

Reality: Every successful enterprise has the key building blocks of (a) product/service development, (b) distribution, and (c) sales. All are vital, but sales is in a class by itself. When practiced by The Master's standards, sales is the connection that fuses an enterprise to people, helps to shape the company's offerings to meet customers' evolving needs, and nurtures its growth over time.

There is no lifeblood in a business that manufactures blankets, packages and ships them to Wal-Mart, but has no real contact with consumers. And no future. Yes, management may pocket the checks, but others will start talking to consumers, understanding that they now want blankets with designer names imprinted on them, and advising Wal-Mart that they need to shift their strategy and their suppliers. Disciplined and flexible as it is, Wal-Mart will make this shift. It does so every day and salespeople make it happen.

Specifically, those salespeople who act as professionals, as advisors, and as drivers of change and growth.

Which brings us to a key question: What is a customer? The traditional view of *a customer* is someone the business serves or sells to. The time has come to reinvent this perspective and adopt a 360-degree model that is simple in its focus and powerful in its impact.

The 360-Degree Customer Experience

The customer is someone we build our business around.

To the extent that they are no longer *customers*. They are members of the family.

Building your business around members of the family, instead of the standard transactional view of serving customers, requires that you make the following transitions in your viewpoint and your actions:

Traditional Way		**Master's Way**
Meet Customer Expectations	vs	Exceed Their Expectations
Satisfy Customers	vs	Thrill Them
Give Customers Everything They Expect	vs	Surprise Them with Gestures of Thoughtfulness
Give Customers Access to Products/Services	vs	Wrap Them in a Cocoon of Care
Be Satisfied if Customers Like Your Product/Service/Company	vs	Make Certain They Fall in Love with Your Product/Service/Company
Close a Sale	vs	Offer Customers a Lifetime of Unique Experiences and Values
Be Willing to Take Customers' Next Orders	vs	Commit to Them

The following chapters will further explore the elements of The Master's way.

As you can see, especially when compared to traditional *selling*, the 360-Degree family member experience is:

- Personal.
- Proactive.
- Perpetual.
- Protective.

Nothing is more powerful than this.

WHY MOST SALESPEOPLE CAN'T SELL

1. They have nothing interesting to say.
2. They cannot present their products and services in a compelling fashion—in other words, as more than just products and services.
3. They believe they have done their job if they get prospects to *like* what they are offering. The fact is, they have to *fall in love* with it.
4. They fail to develop a Power offer that makes what they are selling impossible to refuse.
5. They don't bother to **read** the prospect. They're too preoccupied with the commissions they WON'T earn precisely because all of the focus is on themselves.

II

God Shares His Vision

God never *sells* a product or a service. God holds out an ideal, a standard to achieve, and most important, something to aspire to. Great salespeople learn from this and emulate it.

I remember a day I spent with Bill Gates before he was a household name. Microsoft was just a hotshot business among a thousand hotshot companies in the burgeoning world of information technology. As we strolled the Microsoft campus, Gates was *selling* me on his company. But not by touting his software. He never uttered a word about that. Instead, he waxed poetic about an ideal encapsulated in a vision: His goal of seeing a computer on every desk in every home and office. This is something we take for granted today, but at the time it was a truly audacious goal. And as Gates knew instinctively, it was something far more powerful to sell than computer code.

There is a genuine analogy here to religion, which *sells* us the ability to have meaning in our lives. To experience a force far greater than ourselves. This is what bonds us to God. All too often, salespeople completely ignore the power of a compelling vision and stay focused on a pedestrian product instead of identifying and extolling the true virtues within it.

Consider the salesperson in a furniture store. You walk in, you browse, he sees you out of the corner of his eye, and in a well-practiced pounce, he moves in for the kill.

Salesperson: "May I help you?"
Prospect: "Perhaps. We need a kitchen table."
Salesperson: "Very good. I'm sure I can help you. How much do you want to spend?"

In an instant, the sales hack reduces the potential joy of buying a new kitchen table to a responsibility, a job, a budgeting exercise. With all the opportunity in the world to make this an enjoyable experience, he reduces it to a cold and pragmatic transaction.

But it doesn't have to be that way. Consider Kurt, a furniture evangelist in Stowe, Vermont. (Yes, "evangelist," that's what a great salesperson must be.)

When my son and I walked into Kurt's store on a

snowy February afternoon, he asked if we'd been skiing earlier in the day.

MS: "Oh yes, perfect day on Mt. Mansfield."

And then Kurt connected the dots.

Kurt: "And now you want to find the ideal table for those equally perfect après ski dinners with your family. Am I right?"

MS: "Bingo."

Kurt: "Wonderful. I love to hear that. The greatest thing about skiing is the way it brings families together. You're not really looking for a table, per se, you are seeking the ideal centerpiece for sitting down with the people you love and sharing stories of the great times you have together schussing down that mountain. All of the tables you see here would be great for that, but let me show you an antique table that captures the spirit of what you are after."

Kurt had the gift. Kurt had the insight. Kurt knew **not** to sell me a product. Kurt understood the power, the majestic appeal, of *selling* me love, warmth, and family values. He had a vision and he knew precisely how to share it with me and make it mine. Not only did I *buy* from Kurt that day, but I have done so for the past twelve years and counting. Everyone has inventory; Kurt has something far more precious. He has dreams.

III

People Buy *Trust* Before They Buy *Products*

Salespeople tend to ignore or discount the truism that "it is greater to give than to receive." Or worse yet, they think it has little or nothing to do with their professional lives. After all, as salespeople they have to produce, right? Produce sales and, most important, receive the funds that constitute payment in kind.

Yes, of course, but this need not be—in fact, it should not be—at the heart of what they do. Far better is to find a passion for delivering something of value to others—life insurance, software, vacations, dream homes—and do it with an understanding and a realization of how what they are selling can add to their customers' lives, and the sales, the lifelong relationships, and the bountiful rewards will come with it. Why? Because prospects and customers will be *sold* on **you** and everything else will follow. If they trust you, they will buy from you. If they don't, you will walk away empty-handed no matter how cool or elegant your product may be.

Smith Barney manages part of my money. The point person on my account is what most people would refer to as a *stockbroker*. I know all the slick names the Wall Street firms give these sales folks—financial advisor, wealth consultant—but for the most part they are stock jocks regardless of the fancy terms inscribed on their business cards. I run a marketing firm that has served many financial services companies, so I know how this name game works.

But don't jump to conclusions: The man who serves me at Smith Barney has demonstrated over and over again that he understands the power not of getting but of giving. To me he is not a *stockbroker*. Or a financial consultant. Or a Wall Street wizard. Most of all, and I value this greatly, he is a member of my extended family. Every other firm, every other *stockbroker* can compete for my business, but no one can take his place. I won't give them an inch. I trust him.

Just the other day, he advised me to have my will reviewed. Nothing unusual about that. Many of the men and women who sell financial products do that. It's become part of their script. They make the recommendation, view it as obligation, and then move on to the real reason they came to visit you that day: to sell you commissionable products.

But not my adviser: This was the twentieth or so time he reminded, urged, and cajoled me to have that will reviewed. Why? Because he knows—given that I had it prepared many years ago under different estate laws and dramatically different personal circumstances—that it is likely out of date. He benefits in no way from my having a proper will, except by knowing that he has done the right thing in virtually dragging me to the lawyer's office to get it done. And in spending all of this time reminding, urging, and prompting me to do the right thing, he has given up precious time he could have devoted to *selling*. Instead, he used it to build trust.

When I finally came to my senses and agreed to have my will updated, my Smith Barney guy, my virtual relative, set up the call with the lawyer, joined the conversation, and when the attorney suggested a personal meeting, he insisted on attending.

I know my guy is defined by Smith Barney as a *salesman*. And I know he treats me in the exceptional, caring manner that is his signature, so that I will stay with him and keep my assets invested with him (and stiff-arm anyone who tries to take his place).

But that's not important to me. All I care about emotionally and intellectually is that this man recognizes that a business relationship need not be—should not be—all business. From my perspective, he gives me far more in terms of advice, trust, guidance, and commitment than the value of the commissions I pay to him.

The hackneyed *rules* of salesmanship stress that "time is money" and advise that if you want to be a top gun, allocate your time only to what pays the most. Hold brief meetings with the best prospects, close them in lightning speed, and move on to the next big opportunity. Sounds like timeless wisdom, but it is really a hollow cliché. The real winners in life and in selling know that this hit-and-run approach may generate commissions, but it doesn't build relationships and that without the latter, the enduring rewards fail to materialize.

Barbara Cleary is one of the most successful real estate agents in the upscale community of New Canaan, Connecticut. Barbara has reigned atop the town's brokerage rankings for more than two decades. What is her secret? How does she outsell dozens of other equally ambitious and driven brokers year after year, market cycle after market cycle?

The tin soldiers of selling, the automatons who do it by the book, will tell you it's all about making more cold calls, playing golf until your arms are sore, keeping your nose to the grindstone. But to Barbara Cleary, nothing about the route to sales success is voodoo. Yes, she sells homes, but first and more important, she educates families on the joys of living in a town she truly loves, a town in which she has raised six children, and a town where she believes her clients will discover a kind of heaven on Earth. From the moment would-be buyers walk into her office, Cleary treats them as family members.

"They will be my *neighbors*," she says, "not my *customers*. I will be greeting them on the streets, attending dinner parties with them, joining them on the Christmas Holiday stroll. As I sit with them in my office, I don't feel as if I am selling them a house. I am interested in doing something of much higher value: bringing families to our wonderful town. I know without any possible doubt that this will be the finest move of their lives, that they will experience a kind of joy that is so rare anywhere else. I can guarantee that.

"There are many homes available, but there is only one New Canaan. I think they see my passion—and feel it."

I have witnessed Cleary at work and I can tell you that her evangelical belief in what she is selling is the primary force in her success.

IV

God Makes Guarantees

The scriptures advise that we can have absolute faith in God and that He will return that faith with a bulletproof assurance that His force will be with us, our families, and all of our loved ones for all of our lives.

Consider that the supreme guarantee.

As a *salesperson*, is there a way you can replicate this? Of course, you're not omnipotent, omnipresent, and all knowing. But when you *sell* something to someone, you can be unequivocal about what that product or service will deliver. And this has exceptional power.

"I remember a dark day in my business life," says the owner of a sporting goods equipment company and—as an entrepreneur and CEO responsible for driving his company's growth—a lifelong salesman. "It felt as if I was on the edge of an abyss—I had near zero in my business bank account, my personal wealth was down to the equity in my home, and as far as I could see, I had nothing on the horizon that could turn things around. I was in a free fall, about a hair away from hitting bottom.

"And then I decided to try and pull a rabbit out of the hat. One of my friends worked for Jack Nicklaus. I asked him to please pull some strings, use his connections and his access to the golf legend, and arrange an audience for me with the Golden Bear. I knew that if I could somehow secure the rights to use the Nicklaus name on my product, I could borrow the money to create a new line of Nicklaus-branded products and use this to revive my business by cracking into the big retail accounts that had, to this point, closed the door in my face. It would be my silver bullet.

"As a favor to my friend, Jack granted me the meeting. As I prepared for it, I knew I shouldn't treat this as a sales call. In fact, that I should never again treat any such meeting as a *sales* call. It dawned on me that perhaps my failure to rethink the way I was selling, or worse yet the way I'd always sold, had landed me in the predicament I now found myself in.

"I knew I would have to talk to Jack, not with some plastic elevator speech, but instead from the heart and the soul. From *my* heart and soul. And that I shouldn't try to sell him a hot product line that would make me just another peddler. Instead, I should sell him on me.

"When he walked into the conference room at one of his glorious golf communities—championship moments captured in dozens of black and white photos adorning the walls—I knew even more than I had anticipated that I was in the company of greatness. The guy's aura filled the room. It was to me something that felt at that pedal-hits-the-metal moment, larger than life. At any other time I might have choked, but thankfully at this make-or-break encounter, I was prepared.

"I walked right up to the famed golfer, shook his hand, and seized control of the agenda:

"'Jack, all my life I have played double-A ball. Now I am ready for the majors.'

"I looked squarely in his steely eyes and could tell without a doubt that I had his attention.

"'If you afford me the right to use your name on one of my products, I will pledge my life to making you proud. To treating the Nicklaus brand with all of the quality it deserves. I personally guarantee you that I will view this not solely as a business deal, but also as a personal obligation to demonstrate my commitment and integrity as a human being.'

"We never sat down. The Golden Bear, dressed in a green golf shirt and khaki slacks, looked me up and down for what felt like an hour. Then he asked me to wait outside the office as he consulted with his lawyer. Minutes later he returned, gripped my shoulder but didn't say a word. He didn't have to. I knew by the way he clutched me that we had a deal.

"That one day, that one *sale*, made my year, saved my company, and taught me a life lesson, a *sales* lesson, that has turned my company around:

"Make a guarantee people believe, in great part because you intend to stand behind it, and people will gravitate to you. They will have faith in you."

Unfortunately, this story and the outcome it delivered is atypical. When we humans *sell*, we tend to dilute our message. To add fine print and weaken the selling proposition with 101 caveats. Every one of those wishy-washy clauses diminishes the power of your message and significantly reduces the likelihood of making a sale.

People tend to focus on the big picture issues, but so often what appears to be the little things—a word, an expression, even a subtle shade of attitude—can have a major impact and make or break a sale. Especially when the focus of attention is riveted on the guarantee (specifically, how much the prospect can bank on it).

One encounter I recall brings it all into sharp focus. The CFO of a multinational consumer products company was interviewing each of the Big Four accounting firms with the goal of hiring one of the Goliaths to perform the company's annual audit. With millions of dollars of fees on the table, each of the four contenders were eager to win and were using the only tactic they could think of: touting their financial prowess as superior to that of the other contenders.

After an intensive comparison of the firms' capabilities, the CFO decided that one of the firms would be best for the engagement, providing—and this was a big "if"— that the partner he had been talking to about awarding the audit would make a personal commitment to be the point person in the firm-to-client relationship.

> CFO: "As you know, although you may not want to readily admit it, all of the contenders seeking to perform our audit are superb firms. Great skills, terrific people, and relevant experience. There isn't a clinker in the group!
>
> "That much said, I am leaning toward selecting your firm because of one major factor: YOU. If you pledge to lead the engagement, and I mean really lead it as opposed to being a front man, we can shake on it now and move quickly to a contract."

Between the lines, the CFO was saying, "Give me a guarantee." And the audit partner, the trophy inches from his hands, blew it.

Audit Partner: "Bob, you know how proud our firm would be to serve you and how well suited we are for this engagement. I can't tell you how delighted I am with your selection."

With that, he extended his hand to shake the CFO's and said, "And you have my word that I will try my best to personally serve you."

Try my best! Consider that the polar opposite of a guarantee. In an instant, the CFO recognized that the audit partner was interested in selling him, not serving him, and that his *guarantee* would not be worth its weight in sand. The wishy-washy *guarantee* had DEAL BREAKER written all over it. The CFO showed his displeasure, mumbled an excuse about needing Board approval, promptly called back the firm that had been his second choice, secured the assurance he was seeking from a senior partner there, and closed the deal.

As you think about this encounter, one that occurs thousands of times a day in a multitude of circumstances, remember God never says, "I *may* be your savior." Belief in God and your religion tells you that the promise of His love and support is guaranteed.

So must be yours. It is that powerful.

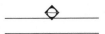

When I was in the hospital for my by-pass surgery, a member of the administrative staff visited my room to conduct a so-called consent. A thirty-something Hispanic woman, who looked as if she'd been brainwashed and stripped of emotions by the hospital bureaucracy, approached my bed, clipboard in hand, all business.

Admin: "Mr. Stevens, I need a few moments of your time."

MS: "Not another stomach injection," I said, half joking, half pleading.

I had been on a painful regimen of pre-op anticoagulants injected into my abdomen twice daily. I was hoping this wasn't the third dose of the day.

The young woman had little to do with the practice of patient care and seemed mystified by my reference to injections.

Admin: "I have to go through your consent forms," she said, stone-faced and eager to get down to the task at hand.

MS: "Let's do it."

Admin: "You will be having a procedure known as by-pass coronary surgery. I must advise you that there is significant risk associated with this procedure. I need you to sign this consent form acknowledging that there is a five percent chance you will have a serious complication, including the possibility of a stroke or death."

With that, she placed a pen in my hand and put the clipboard on my lap.

Let's think about what occurred here. A stranger advised me, matter of factly, that I could become a vegetable or abruptly die on the operating table. To her, it was just another duty to perform, another day at the office. Think of it as hospital music. It goes with the sounds of groaning and crying that are part of the fabric of the place.

Anyway, the young woman consents me, and I sign the appropriate form with the understanding that what she does and says is part and parcel of the system. And I return to the book I am reading, waiting for visiting hours to begin.

The next day one of the cardiothoracic surgeons, who will actually cut through my sternum, split my upper torso in half, and create a new arterial system around my heart, stops by to talk. Instantly, I recognize a difference between this physician and the administrative staffer more profound than their educational credentials or place in the hospital hierarchy: He is a *salesman* and she is the polar opposite. He knew the power of the guarantee.

Dr. Smith: "How are you doing, Mark?"

MS: "Actually quite good, although I'd love to get this waiting game over."

Dr. Smith: "Well, you are just about there. At this time tomorrow, Mark, you will be out of the OR and on your way to recovery."

That's when I confided in him a concern and a confidence that had been brewing inside of me ever since I was thrown into the back of the ambulance and sent weaving through New York traffic on my way to the hospital.

MS: "If you make sure I open my eyes at the end of the surgery, I will fight my way back to the recovery you are promising me."

With that, Dr. Smith, central casting's ideal for a major-league surgeon or a NASA astronaut, put his hand in mine and issued the only pronouncement I wanted to hear: "Mark, you'll open your eyes. I GUARANTEE it."

Trumpets blared. The clouds parted. Sun shone into my room. I was in the hands of a master.

V

It's Not the *Product* That Sells, It's the *Provider*

Everything you have ever learned about selling is likely wrong. *Taught* to you by people—sales managers, gurus, seminar hosts, professors—who have never sold anything to anyone. In fact, they would likely find a way to discourage the most eager prospect from buying what they want to buy. So given the failure to sell, they decided to *teach* and chances are you've taken the class.

Now it's time to erase it all from your minds.

What masquerades as sales training is often a set of flawed practices passed along from generation to generation, from person to person, sometimes with the best intentions, but best intentions don't get people to write out checks.

Those who are really experts at selling don't devote their careers to talking about it. Instead, they do something the sales seminar guys are unable to do: They just sell. Quietly and silently, without fanfare or bragging, they

---

amass customers, romance them for life, and in the process, generate a windfall of revenues and commissions.

Chances are you have spent too much of your time *learning* from the pretenders. I remember "the wonder years" moment when I first saw *the teaching as opposed to selling disconnect* in action. It was the summer of my high school junior year. The typical employer was paying kids like me $50 per week for the classic grunt work of busing tables and mowing lawns. But I noticed a classified ad promising the "right" high school kid $150 per week for a "challenging but rewarding summer job." Music to my eyes. I called the number in the help-wanted ad, virtually sprinted to the company's offices, and found that the "rewarding summer job" called for selling magazine subscriptions, door to door—not bad for that kind of rich increase over the standard summer job paycheck. But there was a catch: I would be going door-to-door in Harlem, not quite friendly turf at the time for a lily-white guy.

Still, I jumped at the offer because I needed the money and was cocky enough to think I would find a way to get by in a war zone if I had to. Hey, I was sixteen and immortal! Surprise, surprise, I landed the job (or was I the only applicant thick-headed enough to take it on once it was clear "the right high school kid" would have to parachute into enemy territory?).

The boss of this dubious enterprise—they called it Metro Educational Enterprises, or some such nonsense—fashioned himself a prince of sales. Some prince! The image of him sitting at a steel army-surplus desk with half-eaten sandwiches piled up around him is still burnished in my memory. Anyway, he decided he would teach me the ropes before I ventured out into the mean streets. Not, I am sure, to provide for my safety, but to raise the odds that I would come back each day with copious orders for *Jet* and *Ebony* magazines.

A classic Damon Runyon figure, he appeared to be an alcoholic (something about the way he slurred his words, downed Dixie Cups of Jack Daniels for breakfast, and wore a grey felt hat in the middle of the summer), but wow! he was going to *teach* me the ropes. How lucky could a high schooler get?

"Listen kid, you can make more moola than you ever dreamed of this summer. Sell more than fifty subscriptions a week and I'll pay you mucho bonuses on top of that très generous salary we're forking over.

"But listen up: If you want to get your hands on that green stuff, you have to allow me to teach you and pay attention to me. I know from which I speak.

"Here's how you do it: Don't sell magazines to the people you'll be calling on. Well, what I mean is, of course you have to sell the magazines, but focus instead on the sweepstakes you will be generous enough to enter them into just for talking to you. That will get you in the door and then once you're inside their little abodes, they'll buy and buy and buy . . . because they'll think the more subscriptions they pay for, the more the odds of winning the sweepstakes will shift in their favor. And if they aren't smart enough to connect the dots, kid—these won't be the sharpest pencils in the box you'll be dealing with—connect it for them.

"Repeat after me: Buy more, better chance of winning. Buy more, better chance of winning. They'll eat it up, kid. Think of it as money in the bank."

It didn't take me more than a few days on the job to realize the prince of subscription sales (a) never sold a magazine in his life, (b) had never stepped foot in Harlem, or (c) both. Legendary Hollywood producer William B. Mayer once said, "Make a bad movie and people will stay away in droves." The approach I *learned* from the prince was now *my bad movie*. Sweepstakes? I tried to get my prospects excited about this, of course. Remember, I was sixteen, green, and had never really sold in my life. So I took the prince's advice at the outset. But, true to form when you take the sales *teacher's* advice as gospel, I flopped: I didn't get a soul to open the door. So I switched gears and told my prospects I wanted to talk to them about learning, education, and wisdom. I'd never spent time in the inner city before, but I figured the clichés I'd heard about poor black people were the product of racism and that if I talked to my prospects about the universal dreams everyone has for their families, I would surprise them and engage them in a real conversation about the genuine value of what I was selling.

When I announced at the door that I was there to talk about education, the people not only let me in, they made me lemonade and offered me fresh-baked cookies. And most important, they listened as I described the magazines I was selling and how they could use them to educate themselves and their children on news, history, and culture. In the process, I made a guarantee—that the learning, education, and wisdom encapsulated in the magazines I was selling was assured to pay real-life dividends because those who read are those who grow and achieve.

I guaranteed them—because I believed it—that there was no better gift they could give to their families.

I made $400 a week that summer. I also made friends and gained valuable insights into *salesmanship* that have stayed with me throughout my career and proven themselves over and over again:

- When you try to fool people, you are only fooling yourself.

- When you demonstrate timeless value, people will embrace your offering and advise others to do the same.
- When you can make a bulletproof guarantee, you will have an abundance of customers.

I also learned through my summer of trial and error how and why the majority of so-called *salespeople* fail to sell: They think it's the **product** that counts, when it's the **provider** that cements the sale.

Let's personalize this. Do you sell a *good* product or service? If you say "No," you should lobby for improvement or change jobs. Selling something of value can often be challenging enough; selling something inferior or defective can create an insurmountable challenge. If you say "Yes," I say, "Congratulations, you are off to a good start." But before you take a bow, allow me to remind you that a *good* product or service is simply the price of admission for gaining entrance to the sales arena.

With so many offerings to select from in virtually every niche—cars, cheese, jeans, computers—prospects will not settle for *good* because *good* isn't good enough. They want and expect an extra dimension and, in every case, that should be YOU. More than product bells and whistles, more than service features, people want to buy from and work with a provider, a salesperson, a relationship builder who adds an exponent to the process of satisfying needs and wants.

Let's put this in perspective again by reflecting on the power of God. When people proclaim their faith, it is not based primarily on a love of church rituals, prayers, or psalms. Behind all of this—breathing life into it and making it rich, truly rewarding, and exhilarating—is The Provider. It is God.

None of us should ever aspire to God's exalted position. There is but one God. But we can learn from The Master. In fact, I believe strongly that He wants us to learn from the teachings of the religions that celebrate Him. And furthermore, that He has established a standard of ethics and of exceptional behavior to serve as a model for all of our endeavors. Think of it as a blueprint to follow.

As we seek to learn from The Master, we should think of why He is adored. It has nothing to do with a product or service, it is because we believe God is:

- Great.
- Loving.
- Accepting.
- Generous.
- Moral.

None of these attributes are flashy, trendy, exotic, or

expensive. Quite the opposite, they represent the staff of life, simple goodness and inner beauty that is so rare in our world that when we see it we are awed by it. We embrace it and give ourselves to it.

I remember a meeting at a client's offices in Palo Alto, California. The chief operating officer happened to mention that the company recently unveiled a new sales process run by an elite group of former software writers and one of the members of the sales team was writing more business than any of her ten colleagues combined. I admire great salespeople, love to watch them work, so I asked the COO if he knew her secret to success.

> COO: "Her secret? I'm not sure you'd call it a secret, Mark. She is such a beautiful woman that people just love to buy from her. Sometimes, I think they don't even know what she's selling."

An exaggeration of course, but I got the point . . . or I should say, I thought I did.

Weeks later, the COO set it up for me to see the sales star in action. I would meet her in advance of a prospect meeting in St. Louis. We were going to have breakfast together, talk a bit, and then head over to the meeting. As I looked across the hotel dining room where we were to rendezvous, I had my eye out for a natural beauty, the kind of showstopper the COO described. And sure enough, I spotted a gorgeous young woman dining alone. As I approached her table, she looked up from the *Wall Street Journal* she was reading, rather surprised and a bit put off as I inquired, "Pardon me, but are you Donna?"

"Sorry, but you have the wrong person."

Barely finishing her words, she buried her face back in the *Journal* and pretended I didn't exist.

Mistake acknowledged, I found the hostess and asked if a Donna had inquired about a Mark Stevens. "Oh, yes, she's been waiting for you. Right this way, Mr. Stevens."

Within moments, I was seated beside the polar opposite of the kind of woman my mind's eye had painted of Donna. The real sales star was not physically attractive in the least: slightly overweight, prominent nose, expansive forehead. I wondered how anyone could think of her as beautiful. And then she smiled . . . and her face lit up the room. A nanosecond later she talked, and her voice was honey. And as we dined, I was swept into her charms in a way that had rarely happened to me before. There was a primal beauty that emerged from what was clearly a true and tender person with heart and brains and a desire to look through your eyes and into your soul. Without saying a word, she made me feel as if she wanted to know me and for me to know her. Donna knew instinctively that the **product** was nowhere near as important at the **provider.** Thousands of others could sell you software. She was *selling* a relationship, and you believed instantly that it would be a relationship for life because you believed Donna was:

- Great.
- Loving.
- Accepting.
- Generous.
- Moral.

And when Donna guaranteed her customers that something would exceed their expectations, they believed it (as did she), and they bought time and time again.

VI

There Is No Such Thing as BAD

God tells us that anything we may perceive as **BAD** is really **GOOD**!

This is not a manipulation or a fairy tale. It is a positive way of viewing the yin-yang of life and to benefit from the power and solace of faith. God makes us see that what appears as bad or even catastrophic at first blush is part of the continuum of existence and, in many cases, a joyous transition.

Think of just some of the ways religion provides a deeper vision, a faith, that *bad* is really *good*:

- You believe life is wonderful, a precious gift. But death (to the faithful) can be even better. Immediately after Pope John Paul II died, one of the cardinals attending his funeral in Rome remarked: "God has whispered in his ear and asked him to join the Lord in heaven."

Does that sound bad? Of course not. It is comforting and helps us to see within the context of our limited human knowledge that death need not be viewed as a dead end. It can be seen as a new beginning, a time for closer proximity to the Lord.

- When a loved one dies, you mourn. But instead of indulging in endless grief, you can take comfort through faith that the person is simply passing from one dimension to another and, in the process, moving from the trials and tribulations of human life to a place of rest and eternal peace.

In God's language, no one is ever being obliterated from the face of the Earth. We are simply and wonderfully being transported to another, even better, place.

- If you *sin*, God teaches that you can absolve yourself of the consequences of committing wonton acts by admitting them and engaging in repentance. And as you emerge at the other end of the sin-to-redemption continuum, God blesses you as a better person for admitting the error of your ways.

Certainly, to sin is not an act to be proud of. But neither is it reason for external damnation. The *bad* of sinning can be turned into the *good* of redemption.

It all boils down to this key principle: Religion tells us that if we have faith in God, everything will be comforting and reassuring.

When I was child, I was warned by my buddies in the neighborhood that there was a heaven and a hell. And that the latter was a horrifying place with fires burning and the devil inflicting great pain and misery. The vision was more horrible than I could bear to think about. Each time it came into my mind, I tried to squeeze it out, but there were nights lying in my bed alone when the specter of hell terrified me.

And then suddenly, blissfully, I was liberated from the fear. One evening shortly before Halloween, my parents sat on the edge of my bed and gave me the greatest news bulletin I'd ever heard: "Mark, there is no hell. Not to those who have faith in God. All of *us*, the believers, we go to heaven."

I felt the greatest sense of relief in my life. I thought to myself: "All I have to do is believe in God and the door to heaven will be forever open to me. There will be no hell for Mark."

Was there anything to ponder? Would I choose whether or not to believe in God? Would I risk walking the route to hell if believing in God meant I was saved from damnation? No way! I was believing in God for the rest of my life. Period. No questions asked. Throughout my childhood, I'd heard some of my friends question, "Do you think there's really a God?" I have to admit, sometimes I wondered. But the moment my parents advised me that belief in God would save me from hell, those days were over. My parents didn't put *the fear of God* in me, they put *the love of God* in me. If I showed faith, the Lord would protect me forever, and I felt extraordinary peace and relief for it.

God's guarantee is not conditional. It has no fine print. Nothing for lawyers to litigate about. Believe in God, demonstrate your faith, be a person of the Lord and you will **not** go to hell. The *bad* will turn to *good*. You will go to heaven. Why would anyone say "No" to that?

Interestingly, salespeople who fail to learn from The Master offer the opposite of this *bad-to-good guarantee*. Inadvertently, but no less damaging than if it were intentional, they talk customers and prospects into *not* buying what they are selling by saying everything may not be all right. In effect, they take their prospects and customers on troubling journeys from good to bad.

- Good-To-Bad: Consider this common pitch from a financial services salesperson seeking to sell a young couple on an investment plan.

"I suggest that you build a portfolio of stocks to serve as a financial engine for your future. This is the best way to take responsibility for the well-being of yourself and your family."

Sounds fine and certainly based on wise advice, but then comes the deal breaker: "Of course, you know the market could crash at any time."

I know that appropriate caveats are required when you are selling many products and services and that this is a healthy part of an ethical process, but the timing in this case, and so many like it, is awful! You must allow the person to absorb the power of your idea before diminishing it and thus pulling the rug out from under it, from under them, and from under your ability to sell a worthy product or service.

Think of it this way: God doesn't say: "Believe in me and *maybe* you won't go to hell."

All you would remember is the *maybe*.

- Good-To-Bad: Then there's the salesperson presenting a breakthrough product to a prospect who is clearly enrapt by its techno features. Just as the prospect is about to buy, the salesperson kills his own deal.

"As you know, this is an excellent product. We take tremendous pride in engineering its performance features

---

that should far exceed your expectations. But, of course, we can't be responsible if you fail to follow instructions. In that case, anything can happen."

What's the rush to shoot holes in the guarantee? To put fear and skepticism in your prospect? To deny them the right to be romanced by the product or service—to marvel at its wonders for a while? Sure, you should be completely truthful and tell all, but everyone can fall in love even though they know there are downsides and risks. Let the love take hold.

- Good-To-Bad: Worst on the list of sales sins is to taketh and then giveth away, often in an instant.

You know the drill: We have all been victims of it. A salesperson extends you a wonderful offer, say a week in Walt Disney World for the entire family, airfare included, for $1,200. Even if you had no intention of going on vacation, you want to seize the offer. It appears too good to pass up. In many ways, this is what really good salesmanship is all about—prompting you to dream about something that was not on your shopping list and getting you to want it and buy it because it will add joy to your life. But instead of assuring you that the surprisingly good deal, like the Disney package, isn't a come-on that's too good to be true, you get a slap-in-the-face confirmation that your skepticism is well founded.

"Of course," the salesman says, "this offer does not apply to holidays or peak periods."

Precisely the time everyone else wants to seize the offer.

You don't have to be a professional salesperson to make this "taketh and giveth away" blunder. As I have noted, from time to time we all have to sell something and unless we learn from The Master we may well fall flat on our face, crawling away without the sale even if what you are doing doesn't appear to be *selling* at all.

Think of how this applies in a marital relationship. On many occasions my wife has asked me—in a playful, romantic moment when she is seeking comfort and total peace of mind—if I will love her forever.

"Yes, my dear, for eternity. We are unbreakable. We are one." Each time I have answered this way, my response has come from the heart.

But when she has questioned ever so lightly, at times I have taketh away—unintentional, but damage done nevertheless.

"How can you be sure that you will always, always love me, Mark?"

"Because you are so deeply embedded in my heart. Of

course, life has a way surprising us at times, but as far as I can possibly see honey . . ."

Hardly the assurance she was looking for. My caveat was completely unnecessary.

Recently, one of my friends, Zack, set out to sell his fellow golf club members on the idea of building a grand new clubhouse to replace the poorly designed and aged structure that stood like an eyesore on the club's sprawling grounds. Although this would be aesthetically pleasing and would elevate the club's stature, it would lead to new assessments for the members—and that is always a hard sell. But my friend, acknowledged throughout the club as the champion for a new clubhouse, was determined to wage the good fight. One warm Sunday during a tennis match, he updated me on his progress.

Zack: "I showed the members renderings of the proposed new clubhouse, developed by an architectural firm with a storied history in creating some of the most beautiful structures of this kind in the United States, Ireland, and Scotland. I mean masterpieces of timeless beauty.

"As I unveiled the renderings, my fellow members were intoxicated. They could see how beautiful their new clubhouse could be. Naturally, I was thrilled at their reaction and at the prospect of leading this fundamental change in the club.

"Building on my case, I argued that we needed a new clubhouse because our facilities no longer held their own against competitors in the community, and as a result, membership was declining. The members recognized instantly that what I was suggesting would be a great enhancement over the current building and I could feel a collective sense of pride sweep across the room. I seemed to have them. It was magic."

Sensing a fork in the road, I interrupted.

MS: "Why do you say you *seemed* to have them? I know your taste is impeccable. They responded favorably to the renderings and how the new designs would transform the club. Did something go wrong?"

Zack slapped his hand across his forehead, as if the shock were first hitting him.

Zack: "Did something go wrong? That's an understatement. It was as if I had snatched defeat from the jaws of victory. Just as the members were caught up in the romance of the stunning structure I was presenting to them, just as they were getting excited by the rendering laid out on the boardroom table right before their eyes, everything went black."

MS: "Black? Why? What do you mean?"

Zack: "As soon as I told them that the budget presented by the architects might prove to be unreliable, that there might be construction overruns, additional budget items, and possibly higher member assessments than the proformas indicated, well the old clubhouse looked just fine again. In a flash, it was romance over. Meeting adjourned."

Zack failed to recognize that it was he who threw cold water on the romance. He who gaveled the meeting to a close. He who put the kibosh on the clubhouse dream.

When you sell anything, remember that first you have to make people fall in love with what you are selling. Only after their hearts and minds surrender to your product or service, really absorb it and commit to it, then and only then should you advise them of the caveats that go with any purchase. Breaking the romantic spell every good salesperson builds before a deal is closed means you'll likely walk away empty-handed. That's because you are saying everything that looks BAD is BAD.

This is not about dishonesty or deception. It is about allowing people to see, to feel, to become immersed in the beauty, the joy, the magic of what you are presenting before you quash the dream with distasteful medicine. Should you tell a family admiring a new home for sale that it could burn down and kill them? Of course not. If there are defects in the structure, tell them what you plan to do to address this but give the prospective buyers a chance to care about the home. Before you throw cold water on the dream.

If negatives must be communicated at some point, do so in a positive light, not to deceive but to put the issues into the proper perspective. If the home has defects, you may state it this way: "These older homes have such character, such graceful architecture, but like this one there is often some structural work to be done. Restoring it is often part of the experience, the joy, of buying a house and making it your home."

What is good can and should be perceived as good. You don't kill that joy simply because it isn't perfect. But that's precisely what *salespeople* do day after day, time after time.

A mistake you will never make if you learn from The Master.

VII

God Makes Us an Offer We Can't Refuse

eligion never says, *"Look folks, we really want you
to attend church and to attend often. So each time you
do, we'll give you a free appliance. Come this Sunday and
you'll go home with a new toaster, compliments of Boston
Methodist."*

The leading religions have always recognized that gimmicks and give-aways cheapen and diminish an offering
as opposed to enriching it and infusing it with tangible
value.

Visit the archetypical trade show and you will see
booth after booth of compelling new products, technologies, and services. But instead of focusing on those mar-
vels of manufacturing and science, the *salespeople* at the
booths are busy handing out squeegee balls and pens that
glow in the dark. Why do they engage in this nonsense?

Because someone decided years ago that the best trinkets equate to the most popular booths and somehow this generates the highest sales. Nonsense. If Einstein was at a science conclave *selling* relativity, should he have handed out a basket of Chinese handcuffs with $E=MC^2$ stamped on the bamboo?

Recently, I attended a conference allegedly dedicated to presenting breakthrough technologies designed to protect civilians and first responders from the threats posed by terrorism. As I walked the aisles, I was struck by (a) the vast array of ingenious devices created primarily by the Israelis and the Americans to sniff out terrorist plots before they could be hatched and protect people from harm in the event the threats turned into deadly reality and amazingly, (b) the complete lack of focus by the salespeople manning the booths on what the brains behind these devices had created. Instead of intelligent discussions about the proper use of protective masks or chemical repellants, I was bombarded with T-shirts, toy guns, and commando berets.

The show was all about life and death (or so I thought upon signing up to attend), but the *salespeople* had all the gravity of punky hawkers at a rock concert.

The great religions of the world know better. They have always recognized that they needed powerful selling propositions to get you to believe, to have faith, to be religious, to come to your church, synagogue, or mosque and pray, not on occasion but as a key ritual of your life. So they make profound offers ("You will not go to hell"), and on the flip side, they reveal the consequences of failing to act on them: *"If you believe in God, if you are a person of faith, you will go to heaven. Guaranteed. If you don't believe in God, you will be a sinner . . . and heaven will be closed to you."*

When you understand and accept this, it is hard to say "No" to God. What can salespeople learn from this?

Henry Ford provides an interesting example. Ford is generally recalled as a manufacturer, creator of the assembly line, and father of the Model T. But more than this, Henry Ford was a salesman. And although he sold motor vehicles, he made more powerful offers to people than cars. He made them offers they could not refuse:

- He promised to free farmers from the loneliness of rural America.
- He promised to bring people together for civic, entertainment, and religious functions that—without the convenience of the automobile—had been beyond their reach.
- He promised to let families see the world (or at least more of it than they could easily see before).

- He promised to open vast new employment opportunities.

Ford was a salesman first and foremost and he thrived because he made people offers they could not refuse. He recognized instinctively that you could say "No" to a newfangled contraption that guzzled gasoline, spit fumes, and jolted you along the dirt roads of America. But you could not just as easily say "No" to an end to loneliness or the freedom to see the world.

Observing this kind of selling in action is inspirational and unforgettable. I remember when one of my firm's clients, a big company that owns and operates ski mountains—asked me to analyze the performance of a salesperson at one of their resorts.

The setting was spectacular: a glass-wrapped pavilion with a stunning vista of the snow-painted mountains adorned with towering evergreens. Inside, a fire crackled in perfect harmony with Christmas music piped through the office's stereo system.

A salesman was seated beside prospective buyers of a time-share plan. A thirty-something couple with a toddler straddled across their laps, they were listening to the salesman wax poetic on the financial benefits of club membership. He cited the facts:

- Less expensive than buying a vacation home.
- Sell your shares back to us at any time.
- Profit as membership fees rise.
- Get more for your dollar than a hotel room.

And on, and on, and on. The more he talked, the more he lost. Why? The salesman's finance-centric approach backfired, prompting the prospects to view his pitch through the eyes of a calculator, and thus to rethink the alleged *benefits* and turn them into *liabilities*:

- But if we buy a home instead of a club membership, we will have real equity.
- It's possible you'll no longer be in business when and if we want to sell our shares back.
- There's no guarantee that membership fees will rise.
- We get amazing deals on hotel rooms from Priceline. That's a much less expensive option than the one you are presenting, and with Priceline we're not locked into anything on a long-term basis.

Although the sales representative didn't recognize it, he was doing *anything but selling*. It was intellectual wrestling with his prospects, and once a salesperson gets into that mode, he has lost his opportunity because great salespeople romance customers, they don't battle them. The guy I was observing had no idea that he had to do far more than make his prospects an offer that added up—it had to be an offer they could not refuse.

Precisely what one of his colleagues, a college student selling on weekends, did as I observed her talking with a smartly-dressed widower in his mid-fifties.

"The best feature of the club is that it serves as a family magnet. Our members tell us over and over again that this is where they spend the most quality time with their children, their siblings, their extended families. More than the skiing in winter, more than the golf and the hiking in summer, more than the charm of the club lodgings, is the fact that it draws you and your family to a place where you can be together. To stop the clock and have the time and the place to be a *family* in every wonderful sense of the word."

There were no rebuttals. No debating over dollars and cents. Within an hour, the recently bereaved gentleman seeking to reconnect with his family agreed to become the club's newest member, and he wrote a $25,000 check to back it up.

The dynamic here was both simple and complex. God makes us offers we can't refuse. They are not nice-to-haves or pleasant surprises or freebees that come with your order. They drive into the heart and soul of what makes people feel love, fear, ambition, joy, comfort, and peace. No one in their right mind can say "No" to these powerful feelings and forces. You can say no—millions do, every day—to toasters, software, flat screen TVs, and McMansions. These are not the offers you can't refuse. Religion, serving in the name of God, has always known and acted on the knowledge that it is precisely these irresistible offers that are the key to success.

You must know and do the same.

VIII

God Is a Story Teller

All major religions are based on scriptures. More than a set of rules, these ancient writings are a series of compelling stories about God, the universe, life, and death. Their power derives from the fascinating ability to present and explain the mysteries of existence in dramatic and colorful fashion.

To the extent that they are no longer mysteries.

I think of this as *story selling,* using the word *selling* in the most honorable sense. And furthermore, I marvel at how powerful it has proven to be over the millennia and how forceful and effective it can be for you. Let's look at this story selling in action: Some years ago, when my boys were young, I stopped into a local hardware store to buy a power drill. We had moved into a century-old home and I had a punch list of repair and renovations to do. The proprietor of the store, an astute salesman, asked how my sons were doing. The boys stopped in now and then to buy odds and ends—nails, glue, tape measures—and he got to know them casually. So he used this acquaintanceship and the knowledge that every dad always wants to chat about his boys as fodder for small talk.

And then boom, he did an 180° and he turned the conversation to *fire*.

Yes, *FIRE*. Specifically, how my home, like every other residence in the quaint hamlet of Chappaqua, New York, that I lived in at the time, is vulnerable to catching fire, endangering the boys I cherished more than anything in the world. And by the way, if I wanted to do something to help to ensure their safety, then darn it if this wasn't the ideal time to buy a $349 safety-escape ladder for my home.

The way the storekeeper was phrasing it, this wasn't a matter of making a sound purchase. No, no, no. This was a matter of life or death. If I didn't take out my Visa card and purchase that ladder, I would be placing my children in mortal jeopardy.

The proprietor was making me an offer I could not refuse. But even more gracefully and powerfully than simply making an offer, he was inserting it in the context of a story. One with a happy or a dreadful ending, leaving me the freedom to write the final chapter. The merchant's superior salesmanship, couched in neighborly concern, left me $349 poorer when I left his store but infinitely more comfortable about the safety of my family. Clearly, not every sales pitch can be linked to a life or death scenario, but telling a story adds immeasurably to virtually every sales situation.

When one of my sons attended Cornell University, a professor began the first day's class by displaying his personal biography on a video screen. Chocked full of exceptional accomplishments—Eagle scout, high school valedictorian, Rhodes scholar, father of two CEOs, and a ranking state department official—it was impressive, yes, but left my son thinking "what a pompous and imperious stuffed shirt."

And then just as his who's who résumé was absorbed by all, he lit up another autobiography revealing the failed side of the same life.

"This, my students, is me too."

> lifelong alcoholic
> disinterested spouse
> insensitive friend
> worshipper of all things superficial

This was the professor's gutsy and ingenious way of telling a story: Everyone has two résumés. And as he went on to explain, the greater the dichotomy between them, the less it is possible to know and trust a fellow human being. True, we all have two résumés, but those who allow themselves to be more transparent on both ends of the spectrum are more genuine and believable. Paradoxically, by revealing what is both attractive and unattractive, they are far more effective in *selling* themselves to us because they gain instant credibility, as did my son's professor.

Superior story selling relies on a few key elements:

- The element of surprise.
- A power of epiphany.
- The ability to entertain.
- A conviction that the story has divined a newly revealed truth.

Whenever I want to mentor the people who work for me—be they salespeople, marketing strategists, creative directors, or the vitally important people who answer the phones and are thus our front line of client service—I avoid the cliché motivators and suggest they view the world through a unique prism: Einstein's. It's a story that has always fascinated me and that I know from experience fascinates and motivates others.

Albert Einstein liked to begin with fantasies, with dreaming of what might be impossible—like children's cartoons—and work backwards to reality. He would lie in his bed and create surreal visions and use his intellect and imagination to figure out how to transform the surreal into the real.

If you begin with reality and try to radiate out to the extraordinary—i.e., what to that point has appeared to be impossible—you will likely be stuck in the predictable, the mediocre, the expected. Think about the Einstein way, the Einstein story, as you *dream* about how to achieve a new level of success in your *selling*. In your life.

IX

God Deals In Exclusives

magine selling toilet paper to Wal-Mart. Yuk.

Why do I say "Yuk"? Well, it has nothing to do with Wal-Mart or toilet paper, per se, but a more more potent issue comes into play.

Here's the crux of the issue: Whenever you are in the role of a salesperson, the last thing you want to do is to offer a commodity. Corn, beans, salt, tax preparation services—these are commodities. Anyone can offer them and quite often the one who makes the sales is the one who offers the lowest price. As a purveyor of commodities, you have little to distinguish you, hardly any leverage in the marketplace, and razor-thin margins.

Another reason to learn from The Master. Religion teaches us that only God can provide us with the blessings that faith in God can deliver with such powerful exclusives as:

- Protection of the Lord.
- Life after death.
- Access to heaven.
- Eternal peace.

It is a closed market: If you want these blessings, you have to turn to God.

Again, as a mere mortal, you cannot shower others with such divine blessings. But you can learn from the principles that compel faith in God.

Think of selling commodities as the exact opposite of dealing in exclusives. When everyone else can sell what you sell, you succumb to the mercy of the market. The customer controls you. If a prospect doesn't like your price or your face or the way you dress, they'll buy from the next vendor of that commodity.

"Time out," you may say, "I sell corn, beans, salt, or tax preparation services. Which means, as you have noted, I sell a commodity. Doesn't that mean I am stuck in low-margin land? That I can never bring real power to my selling? That The Master's principles are irrelevant to me?"

Just the opposite is true. The Master's principles can bring extraordinary value to your work. The idea is to brand your commodity so that it is no longer perceived as just another bushel of corn, can of beans, bag of salt, or tax preparation service. Instead, that it is an exclusive offering only you can provide.

Consider the life insurance business. There are hordes of life insurance agents selling more or less the same product: a contract with a financial services company that promises to pay your heirs a specified sum of money when you die. Such contracts are deemed to be commodities, which is one of the reasons most of the people carrying the card "life insurance agent" struggle to make a living and drop out of the business less than three years after they enter it: exhausted, frustrated, and broke.

At the same time, a handful of superstars carrying a similar business card earn millions of dollars annually selling the same *commodity*. How? By branding what they sell, and what they do, as exclusive.

As anything but a commodity.

These successful people leave their offices every day with the same life insurance products in their bag but with a vastly different mindset about how and why to sell these products to their customers and prospects.

To begin with, the top people never view themselves as **life insurance agents.** So much of what we do and achieve in life is a reflection of how we perceive ourselves and of how others perceive us. The top-producing life insurance people refuse to be **agents** of anything.

They view themselves, and make certain they are perceived this way by others, as intelligent and experienced *financial experts*, whose insights on a wide range of issues from planning for college tuition to providing for a retirement nest egg are viewed as even more valuable than the products they sell. This is their way of transforming what could so easily be treated as a commodity into a highly valued **exclusive.**

When you reflect on it, offering yourself and what you *sell* as an exclusive is the only way to assure your long-term success. Exclusivity means that you:

- Demonstrate and deliver a true and unique value.
- Don't simply sell things, you enhance people's lives.
- Deliver what no one else does in precisely the way you do it.

The choice before you is clear and profound: to sell toilet paper to Wal-Mart as a commodity or to establish yourself as a unique professional who helps people grow their businesses, support their families, achieve their dreams. When you focus on the professionalism factor, you make the point that you are *not* selling toilet paper, you are *selling* economics: You are a force who understands the importance of managing overhead to impose financial discipline and thus maximize the bottom line.

The commodity seller is a peddler; the individual who markets toilet paper as economics is a salesperson in the noblest and finest tradition.

x

God's Loyalty Program Is Second to None

Some years ago I found myself in the lobby of the Fairmont Waterfront Hotel in Vancouver, Canada, at 2:30 a.m. I had been a guest at the hotel many times but on this visit I arrived unusually late. It is my custom to go over my preparation for a meeting within twenty-four hours of the session. That night my timeline was tight, but I was determined to prepare in the customary fashion. So middle of the night or not, I unpacked my bags and headed for the lobby to order a cup of coffee and rethink my strategy for the meeting I would attend in the morning.

This was the first time I had come in contact with the hotel's night staff. Given my frequent stays, the day crew knew me well and generally addressed me by name:

"Good Morning, Mr. Stevens."

"Will you be joining us for dinner this evening, Mr. Stevens?"

"How is your day going, Mr. Stevens?"

What struck me on this particular visit was that the night staff on duty addressed me similarly, even though I had never seen them before. And so I wondered, "How do they know who I am?" Precisely the question I posed to Monika, a slight, red-headed young woman at the front desk. Her answer surprised and intrigued me:

Monika: "Whenever a Platinum member of the Fairmont's President Club is arriving at our property, we circulate a photograph of the guest so that we all can be familiar not only with his or her data profile, but equally important, so that we can match a face to the name. This way we can personalize the greeting."

MS: "That's very interesting. And let me tell you, from the vantage point of experiencing it personally, it makes a big difference. But I'm curious: Where did you get my photograph?"

Monika: "We captured it on the Internet. We go to the person's corporate Website or do a Google search and usually find what we are looking for."

Amazing, I thought. Here is a business that has invested in an architecturally-attractive property with lovely rooms, good food, and a beautiful location. And yet when it comes to attracting a cadre of loyal customers, it doesn't rest on its laurels. It goes to the extent of seeking out photographs on the Web and asking the staff to associate names with VIP faces. The hotel *sells* its best customers, not by advertising or sending brochures, but by leapfrogging this cardboard approach in favor of personalizing its relationship with frequent guests.

How many organizations or salespeople who work for them go the extra mile to attain this powerful form of customer loyalty? To win their customers' hearts and minds? To make an everlasting impression? To demonstrate a level of commitment and personal involvement that vastly exceeds expectations? Very few. The salesperson at my automobile dealer wouldn't know me if I bumped into him even though I buy a $100,000 Mercedes SL from him every two years. The builder who sold me my home for more than $3 million doesn't remember what I look like and probably couldn't call me by name now that I have been living in the house for over six years and he has disappeared from my world. The same for the *salespeople* that I do business with at the supermarket, the clothing store, and the electronics shop.

Even the typical fundraising organization disappoints.

I recently met with the senior staff at the Culinary Institute of America (CIA), a proud institution of higher learning that educates young men and women in culinary skills and prepares them for rewarding careers in the restaurant and hospitality industry. Although I have witnessed the students' passion for the CIA, the administrators advise me that few give back to the school in fund-raising campaigns.

I wondered why, until I discovered that the CIA, like so many of its counterparts in academia, often treats alumni as targets of opportunity as opposed to members of an extended family.

"Do you invite the alumnis to simply get involved with the school after graduation—to join advisory committees and the like—before you petition them for money?" I asked.

"That would be a good idea. Perhaps we should try that more often," is the answer I received.

Why would I have to plant that idea in the leaders' heads? No one wants to be *sold* to be an alumni number, to be viewed as part of a solicitation quota. But this is precisely what schools and many cause-related organizations do: The entities with the most humane mission statements turn out so often to be find-'em-and-grind-'em money machines. Yes, their public personas are grand and

virtuous, but at the human level, their stance, their pos-
ture, and their policy are cold and impersonal.

There is no denying that poor or mediocre service and
the lack of personal connections that emanate from it,
are the norm. Correspondingly, demonstrations of exceptional and the genuine relationship BUILDING that goes
with it, are therefore exhilarating. I have thought about
this for years and, in the process, I have asked myself,
"Who optimizes exceptional service more than the hotel
that trains its staff to greet Mark Stevens by name?" And
I recognized the most profound loyalty I have ever seen,
vastly better than anything served up by Fairmont, Lexus,
or Nordstrom, is the standard of loyalty we can learn from
The Master. He always knows who we are and how we
think and what we do and where we go and what we
need and what we want as well as knowing our dreams,
hopes, goals, and fears. And most important, He loves us
through it all.

I remember when my father died. I was seventeen at
the moment I learned of his death. I was pole-axed, won-
dering if I could go on without the man who had been the
rock of my existence.

For the first few hours of learning the shocking news,
I was numb, bewildered, and so badly frightened, it felt
like I was free-falling at ridiculous speeds. And then mi-
raculously I found my center. I felt that God would see

me through the tragic loss. That He would support my mother, my sister, and me, and that He would see to it that my father would rest in peace. There was no question to me that God would be loyal to my family and me and that He would guide us through this sad and frightening turn of events. I believed, and was comforted by the fact, that if I was weak, strong, or someplace in between, the loyalty of The Master would be unwavering.

Fast forward to today. To your career and your business. And let's make time for a reality check: Do your customers or clients believe they can always count on you? Or do you make a sale, blow a superficial kiss, and move on? Do you ever call just to offer your knowledge and your support with the goal of selling nothing?

If you are like most, the answer is "No."

Think of how shallow that is. Of how it is the opposite of relationship building. Of how it leaves you on a commercial and spiritual treadmill, forced to run even faster to move ahead of the curve because little or nothing you have or do creates enduring good will and loyalty. You are transactional! That is shallow, empty, superficial, and bereft of genuine value. Unlike your relationship with the Lord, there is no reason to be loyal to you, because you are loyal to no one.

How can you change this, moving from the standard and stereotypical salesperson to an inspired and enlightened relationship builder who creates and sustains loyalty? Starting today, take the following actions:

1. Ask yourself what you could do for your customers that would truly touch them. A real estate agent I have met combs the local newspapers for articles about children who have achieved academically or in sports, clips the stories, and sends them with a note to the parents, congratulating them on the kids' achievements.

2. Write a hand-written "thank you" note. Not on e-mail or a form letter. The surprise of receiving a letter that you took the time to write, to think about, and to personalize, speaks volumes about your genuine interest in the customer beyond the funds and the legalities of the transaction.

3. Share news with the customer about a major development in your life, such as the birth of a child. When my landscaper sent me a glowing announcement about the birth of his first daughter, I could experience the excitement and felt as if he was bringing me into his family. A wonderful touch.

This illuminates the reality that loyalty is borne from something far more powerful than frequent flyer points or giveaways. It derives from a state of mind.

All too often, the salesperson is in it for the transaction. For the exchange of dollars. And once that transaction has been completed, the salesperson moves on mentally and physically to the next opportunity. And the next. And the next.

That is terribly shortsighted. By viewing transactions as the building blocks of an enduring business relationship as opposed to an end unto itself, salespeople will be infinitely more successful.

Another way to think about this is to debunk the value of a database. Companies in all industries pride themselves on having "a great database of clients or prospects."

Is this really anything to be proud of? A database is simply a list of names, contact, and purchase information stored in a server. In most cases, it is static. Customers reduced to binary code.

As we seek to learn from The Master, we must recognize that God keeps us tethered to Him through an ongoing relationship. Through meetings of the congregation and through private prayer. Through a continuous unveiling of the mysteries, the wonders of life. Salespeople can adapt this practice by turning the database into a community of people to stay in touch with through the years. Think of this, too, as building and nurturing an extended family.

I remember when my wife and I visited a new housing subdivision on the ocean at Hilton Head Island. The salesman took us through the homes, all of which were artfully designed and opened to stunning vistas of the seas. We weren't ready to buy at the time, but that didn't mean he wasn't willing to let us out of his life. He had our names and addresses and style preferences, but instead of putting this information into a database, he used it to add to his *community*. Since we met that salesman, he has sent us interesting articles about the evolution of Hilton Head, new real estate opportunities, his personal observations of the island, trends in investment values, anecdotes about his family life, and inquiries about ours. He sends us birthday cards. Christmas cards. Thanksgiving cards. We are part of his family. He wants to make a sale, of course, but he has demonstrated a personal touch. He has demonstrated loyalty, and we will be loyal to him. We are now thinking of buying a home by the beach, and when we finally decide to make that purchase, he is the salesperson we will buy from. We will reward his loyalty with our own.

The ironic thing is that companies often talk in terms of how loyal their customers may or may not be. I hear it all the time: "I don't know what's wrong with our customers. We give them everything they want and they're just not loyal to us. They'll buy from the next guy who comes along as if we don't even exist."

"What's wrong with these customers?"

Frankly, it's the other way around. The real question should be, "What's wrong with the salespeople?" When a salesperson nurtures and supports customers (note I say *nurtures* and *supports*, not hounds for more business), people don't leave. They embrace the relationship and are exceedingly loyal to it.

My father was just such a salesman. He didn't love the products he sold (plastic sleeves for photo albums); he loved the people he sold to. And he showed this love with extraordinary warmth and humanity. I remember the time one of his clients became disabled and could no longer work. This meant he was no longer in a position to buy anything from my dad. Other salesmen would write the guy off and move on. But my father would have none of that. He made a point to continue his monthly dinners with the gentleman, took him to Yankees games, and invited him to our home for Thanksgiving where he always introduced him as "my great friend." Dad did the same for those who were able to buy from him, but just because a man suffered a misfortune and was no longer a source of commissions, my dad wouldn't think of casting him aside. And you know what happened: Word of my dad's loyalty to his customers (not just theirs to him) spread throughout the industry, and he was widely viewed first and foremost, not as a salesman, but as a friend. Instinctively, and out of love, he changed the classic rules of selling, and he was adored and rewarded for it—spiritually and financially.

The sales guides written by head-in-the-sand gurus won't tell you this because they don't see it, but selling out of love and passion, and the rewards that come from it, go hand in hand.

When my dad died at age forty, more people attended his funeral (their *friend*/their *salesman's* funeral) than I had ever seen gather in one place in my life. The love he exuded came back to embrace him.

XI

God Welcomes Everyone

I t was a raw March morning in Vermont. One of those near-spring days that makes no attempt to reflect the calendar or the cosmic order of the seasons. The steely grey skies and the bite in the wind said that for the time being it's still winter, and it will be a long time before the local men have to take their fish houses off the frozen lakes.

The outright stubbornness of the seasons is one of the charms of the Green Mountain state. My family and I owned a vacation home there for years and I spent as much time as I could skiing, hiking, and simply driving around admiring the simplicity of the clock-stands-still fashionless and timeless beauty of the place.

On this particular frosty dawn, I happened upon a charming little church, perched confidently on a bluff overlooking a pristine lake guarded on all sides by towering pine trees. Nothing terribly unusual here: Hundreds of quaint churches dot the Vermont landscape and speak volumes about the early settlers and the faith they wove into so many of America's communities. Sometimes, tossing aside the history books and simply seeing how the nation's towns are composed, opens a window to a clearer and more powerful lesson than traditional education can provide.

Such as the lesson I learned from the wonderful church that enchanted me and riveted my attention this March day in Vermont. A simple hand-painted sign was mounted on its front lawn:

Sinners Welcome

What a powerful statement. What a generous greeting. What an exceptional thing to volunteer! Sinners—yes, YOU, the ones who acknowledge your fall from grace, come right in and join us. We won't simply let you in. We will "welcome you with open arms." To our family, our congregation. To receive the blessings of our God.

This is exceptionally powerful because it is so rare. In virtually everything we do in life, we are so fast to be critical, to be exclusive as opposed to inclusive, to hold ourselves superior to others and reject them as unworthy of our love and respect. But this church exudes a kindness, a generosity that is deeply moving because it is so rare and so *religious* in the truest sense of the word.

The question is: Can this obscure but remarkable Vermont church and the others like it in quiet communities across the nation serve as a role model for salespeople? For businesses? And for all of us in our careers and personal roles?

For starters, do businesses do anything remotely like this? Do you see a sign outside your Bank of America branch declaring: Deadbeats Welcome? Of course not. Because banks want borrowers who will pay their bills. But wait, it's not that simple. Do churches want congregants who will steal, rape, or destroy? Do they want to be known as a refuge for sinners? Of course not. But they are willing to do something The Master has always advocated: Give people a chance to prove that, with the proper guidance and the opportunity to capitalize on a second chance, they can be respectable human beings and perhaps wonderful additions to the congregation and the community at large.

God gives everyone a chance to redeem him or herself. Surely not all sinners prove worthy of the Lord's generosity, but millions do. All of us are sinners at one time or another and most of us take the opportunity to redeem ourselves. And we are grateful, tremendously so, for the opportunity to do so.

Wouldn't we feel this way about a business, a salesperson, that is equally generous and open-minded? Consider the salesperson who accepts those rejected by all others because of the narrow-minded view that they are tainted forever by their past behavior. That salesperson would have the opportunity to amass an extraordinary base of the most thankful and loyal customers. Think about that sign again, **Sinners Welcome,** and ask yourself how you can extend a second chance to those who are spurned by your competitors. And even more than that, to demonstrate a generosity of spirit to all you come in contact with. The rewards are likely to come to you in ways you could never imagine when you do business by the impersonal, take-no-risk-on people Management 101 book.

I learned about the power of forgiveness in a very personal way.

When I was a senior in high school I decided to make the transition from a kid who held down the usual list of waiter/lifeguard/caddy odd jobs to a kid who would be an entrepreneur. No Silicon Valley ambitions here; I simply decided to spend my winter school break selling Christmas trees. The magazine job had given me sales experience that I now wanted to apply in a small venture of my own. Once I made the decision to go into the tree business and had my financing lined up (a $150 loan from my father), things fell into place quickly. I rented space at a local Texaco station in Bayside, New York, bought a truckload of trees from a wholesaler, asked my sister to make me a few cardboard signs, and whammo I was an Horatio Alger in-the-making.

Even though my tree venture was the tiniest of enterprises, it felt great to be in business for myself. And I enjoyed selling trees to bright-eyed families, especially the little kids, beaming at the prospect of bringing my trees—natural, wonderful-smelling symbols of Christmas—into their homes.

But one thing bothered me. Now and then a few people would come around, look at the trees, talk to me, and then wander off without buying anything. I could see that they wanted a tree, had their dream tree picked out, but would leave empty-handed—and I felt, instinctively, empty-hearted.

I told my dad about it.

Father: "There is really no mystery, Mark—they can't afford a tree."

MS: "How do you know, dad?"

Father: "Years of experience. Also, I've been in their shoes. Not when it comes to Christmas trees, but I know what it feels like to walk away from the bake shop too poor to buy a cookie."

MS: "Something about it feels at odds with the Christmas spirit."

My dad thought for a moment and then he demonstrated why I thought he was the smartest man in the world.

Father: "Mark, when you see the next person you believe is truly in the can't-afford-it category, who would love to buy a tree from you but just doesn't have the money, invite them to take a tree home and suggest they pay you when they can. Just write down your name and phone number on a sheet of paper and tell them you know they just forgot their wallet and that they'll be good for it."

My father's advice delighted me from the moment I heard it. I wanted to make money that winter and I wanted to get paid for my trees, but his words, his advice, were soothing. It just felt right.

Over the next week or so, I gave away about ten trees. It wasn't easy to do. Each person resisted at first, protesting that they had no need for charity and were simply not ready to buy a tree yet. But with a sensitivity and diplomacy I had never displayed before, I convinced them to accept my "loan."

The great epiphany was that these turned out to be the most satisfying *sales* I'd ever made. In due time, six of the ten sent me money, each with a note or a Christmas card, one as late on March 17 (I'll never forget the date). Another sent me a photograph of his family gathered around the tree; an elderly woman added three crisp dollars to the amount due, her gift to me.

Financially, I did okay that Christmas, earning about $75 for my long holiday working the frigid streets of Queens. But the trees I gave away, all ten of them, made me feel rich and successful and more than that, like a person who had built a relationship with his community.

Most interesting, one of the people who never paid me that year looked me up two years later, by happenstance soon after my father died. He told me that he had never forgotten me, how I had saved that Christmas for him and his wife, and that after a bout with alcoholism and bad luck that claimed his business and his bank account, he was back on his feet and wanted to offer me a job. Given that my family and I were now broke and in desperate need of money, I started selling shoes at the man's retail store and the connection between us proved to be a lifelong bond unlike any I have ever had with anyone else.

XII

God Makes House Calls

Richards is a family-owned business, an upscale clothing and jewelry boutique situated like a local monument in the moneyed enclave of Greenwich, Connecticut—a bedroom community for Wall Street's financial engineers. But Richards is more than a luxuriously stocked and amply appointed retail establishment. It is a phenomenon. Just slightly larger than the average Main Street emporium and a fraction of the size of a Nordstrom, Richards is not a store—it's a juggernaut.

You may be thinking: "There must be something special about Richards. It must be blessed with a set of special qualities that enables it to outperform virtually every store in its class." You're right, there is, but in all likelihood that special something is not what you are thinking: At first blush, it can prove to be a mystery.

Drive around the store a dozen times, walk through

its retail sales floors from front to back, and you won't see that special quality. That's because it's not the brick and mortar, the blond woods and stainless steel displays, or the luxury goods that make the difference. It's all in the way Richards serves you, which is their version of *selling*. An important part of this rests with the fact that Richards makes house calls.

When I was home recovering from heart surgery, my salesperson at the store, Arlene, learned of my situation and correspondingly of my need for a dose of TLC. Knowing precisely what I liked, she plucked a gorgeous deep-blue Italian cashmere sweater off the shelves and had it hand-delivered to my home as a gift. Given my state of mind at the time and the lovely surprise that was presented in a Richards gift box, it was the nicest sweater I'd ever received. How it looked on me didn't make the slightest difference.

This act of kindness was not at all unusual for Richards. It is built into the company's service culture that manifests itself in exceptional ways. If a customer really needs something and needs it fast but the store happens to be closed, management will leave home at any time of day or night, bring the keys, and open up for you. In an instant, one of the most successful clothing establishments in the world becomes your personal closet. Place a call to the customer hotline and CEO Jack Mitchell, himself, may be at your disposal. Virtually every other store would respond to your call for help with a recorded message reminding you that the doors are locked and they won't reopen until regular hours. Regular hours? Think about that. We all take this preposterous concept for granted, but *regular hours* really means a customer's urgent needs are our concern only when we are on duty. It is a poorly-camouflaged way of saying, "We run this business to accommodate the schedules of management and employees, not customers."

What does this have to do with salesmanship, and more so, how does God figure into this equation?

Well, you can think of Jack Mitchell as a *merchant*, and you would be right, but hiding behind that rather benign word lies the fact that a merchant is someone who sells you things. But Jack Mitchell is more than a salesman . . . he is a salesman extraordinaire. Just visit his retail habitat any Saturday and observe him working the floor, making suggestions (advising me that "those brown suede loafers are the most comfortable shoes you can put on your feet"), orchestrating his sales team, and always standing out from the crowd, instantly identifiable by the iconic tape measure draped around his neck.

Great salespeople never have to be pursued. They come to you. They are there whenever and wherever you need them. They make themselves omnipresent. They provide you with multiple ways to contact them, they contact you when you expect it and when you don't, and they never tell you, "Come back in the morning." Nor does God. Whenever and wherever you want God, you can find God.

Some years ago, I decided that having my father's gravesite relegated to a cemetery located off an exit ramp of the Long Island Expressway fifty miles from my home was hardly a fitting resting place for the most important man in my life. So I moved him. Given that I often hiked at the Audubon Society's nature preserve in Greenwich, I was familiar with the tranquil and timeless beauty of the place and how it was a haven for lovers and families. What a life-affirming idyll that would make for my dad, always so full of life himself.

Driven by a sense of renaissance, I approached the Audubon Society to create a memorial for my father in a wooded santuary beside an apple orchard. On a glorious May morning, I invited family members to anoint this memorial with love. I gave a brief but emotional talk and then, quite unexpectedly, guest after guest—members of my dad's immediate and extended family—came forward to talk, sing, and cry. My two amazing sons, who had never met their grandfather, talked of the beautiful impressions they had of him and the pleasure it gave them to think that he would be resting in a place that can only be described as heaven on Earth.

I visit my dad regularly, often seeing young families sitting on a teak bench that symbolizes his memorial, and I think, "God's presence is here. He doesn't demand that I visit a house of worship to be with Him. No, not at all. God makes house calls."

The point is: No one wants to worship a remote and inaccessible God. We must feel and experience His presence wherever we are, whatever we do. We must be confident that He is omnipresent, all-knowing and all-loving.

As we all recognize, no salesman can be even remotely akin to God. But we can learn from The Master. Specifically, no one wants a remote and inaccessible salesman. We want the buoyant, hearty, confident, sensitive person who sells you the state-of-the-art telecom services for your business, not to cash the check and walk away. Instead, we want him or her to stop by unexpectedly, confirm that all is well, and manage service problems, even though others might say, "That's another department." We want him or her to happily provide cell and home telephone numbers and make it clear that no call at any time is ever an inconvenience nor an invasion of privacy.

Like Jack Mitchell standing proudly in front of Richards with the tape measure around his neck, we want him or her to be there. Everywhere.

XIII

God Listens But Never Speaks

Sometimes, we believe what we want to believe even if we know in the back of our minds that it's all just rubbish.

Think of the standard-fare pabulum doled out as *advice* by sales gurus. One of their so-called secrets-of-the-trade focuses on the importance of creating an *elevator speech*. In case you are fortunate enough to have been insulated from this gobbledygook or have, based on knowledge or instinct, shown it the exit door in your brain, it is supposed to be a little speech you refer to en route to see a prospect. Think of it as a cookie cutter mini-speech that, as the gurus tell it, will provide you with just the right words to cast a magic spell when you wind up face to face with the prospect. As myth has it, this will succinctly capture the wonders of your product or service and so captivate your prospect that the sale will be all but inevitable. Money in the bank.

Well, I say toss that Pollyanna daydream in the waste bin. And then put a lid on it. And, if you haven't already, forget you ever heard it. Here's why:

- When you see a customer or a prospect, you have to demonstrate clear and unmistakable passion about what you are selling. If you have passion about it, do you need to robotically read about it from a crib sheet? Of course not. Reliance on an elevator speech should serve as a wake-up call that you need to sell yourself first before you seek to sell anyone else, and once you have done that, you don't need to do anything in the elevator but smile with confidence.
- Remember that confidence is the polar opposite of a canned spiel: It is alive and contagious.
- The same *speech* doesn't work for everyone. In fact, effective selling has nothing to do with speech making. Speech making is about you and selling should be about the customer.

Let's turn this thought to God. Those of us who have faith in God believe that He listens to us. He doesn't sit us down and subject us to elevator speeches, to the canned messages He wants us to hear. Just the opposite, He is open to OUR prayers.

So are *you* a speech maker or a person who listens and delivers?

The need to establish your role quickly and decisively is vital for salespeople to be effective. Particularly at those moments in time we should be listening to our customers and prospects so that we truly understand what they want and need (and what they would want if we have the vision and the tenacity to move ahead of the curve and develop it). Then when we speak and act, it is with the power to serve their needs. And we can present a compelling case for what we believe in knowing it is not plucked from thin air (think "elevator speech") but from genuine desire to deliver something of value and importance. Something we are passionate about.

- The ability to get ahead of the curve that I referred to above is vitally important. In many cases, people have a need but cannot imagine a solution for it. Only by listening and thinking and strategizing can great salespeople develop imaginative solutions to those needs and reap enormous rewards in the process.

Think of Apple's Steve Jobs, one of the greatest salespeople in history. Jobs' stroke of genius in creating and marketing the iPod did not come from a specific customer request. The world needed a way to legally download music from the Internet. There was a universal desire, but no clear way to satisfy it. Not until Apple unveiled it in the form of the iPod. By listening first, thinking, and then talking more with action than words, Jobs revolutionized the music industry, sold millions of iPods as fast as they could be manufactured, and added zeros to his extraordinary personal wealth.

Small-time salespeople believe success is based on magic tracks, gimmicks, and clichés built around the idea that the hand is faster than the eye. But the fact is, great *selling* is complex and profound, genuine, and visionary.

So, fast talkers of the world, remember: Whenever you are tempted to write an elevator speech, God listens but never speaks.

This is another powerful reflection of the fact that (a) God is the greatest salesman of all time, and (b) based on the commonly accepted view of salesmanship, God is not a salesman at all. Not an iota of what is standardly viewed as salesmanship is embedded in God. Which makes God the perfect model for salesmanship.

What do I mean by this seemingly paradoxical view?

Simply that God, or I should say the powerful religions that celebrate Him, follows none of the classic 101 selling methodologies that purport to guide but actually detract traditional salespeople from achieving their goals.

Every one of us mortals can detect the standard-issue salesperson approaching from miles away. It's the smell of selling that begins as a faint scent and intensifies to an unmistakable odor. But what the *sales machines* of the world fail to recognize is that no one wants to be SOLD. It is all-too reminiscent of the hunter/quarry contest: Find a prospect, place him in your crosshairs, put a ribbon on your product or service—and sell, sell, sell.

At the other end of the spectrum, The Master holds out an ideal. Paints a picture. Makes a promise. Suggests that you aspire to a state of mind, of spirit. All too often, salespeople never come close to anything spiritual and limit themselves to being sellers of stuff.

Precisely why salespeople are rarely respected. Although they may shrug off *respect* as a commission you can't take to the bank, this is myopic: Respect is a critical prerequisite to making sales!

XIV

God Never Holds a Sale

magine seeing this billboard on the interstate:

CONVERT TO CATHOLICISM:
CHRISTMAS SPECIAL
ONE-WEEK ONLY
$100 OFF PER FAMILY MEMBER

Does anyone select a religion because one is cheaper than another? Do you buy faith on the basis of price? Does God discount His services? Absolutely not. So why do salespeople resort so quickly to diminishing the value of what they are offering by packaging it on the basis of low price? Could it be because they have little faith, little passion, little confidence in what they are selling? Absolutely yes.

All of us comparison shop for some of the products and

services we buy. Not because we are cheap or shrewd, but because the salespeople who have the least to gain from it train us to do so. They are quick to use low prices to capture us as customers. By this very act, they demonstrate their ineptitude. The best way to see this is to consider the cases where low price never figures into the equation.

Consider Irene. A kind and loving woman, she comes to my home every day to walk my dog while my wife and I are at work. What does she charge for this? Frankly, before I wrote this book, I had no idea. Not because I am oblivious to our family expenses, but because everything I know about Irene gives me instinctive faith that her fees are fair.

To check my instincts, I asked my wife, who informed me that Irene charges us $500 per month. Could I find a dog-walking service for less? I haven't tried, but my gut tells me I could get a high school kid to do it for $200 or so. Why don't I pursue this less expensive option and pocket the savings? Because the issue is not one of economics. And before we rush pell-mell to the dollars and cents of things, it is important to take pause. In this case specifically, and as a metaphor for so many other circumstances like it, Irene is technically a *dog walker*, but in reality she is a *dog lover*. Specifically, she shows my wife and me in a thousand ways that she loves our Golden Retriever, Blue. Shall I replace Irene, the Blue Lover, with Joe, the Bargain Walker, to save $300 per month? Not unless I can put a price tag on love (which, of course, I can't). Irene never sold me her services on the basis of price. Nor has Arlene, who sells me most of my clothing. Or Vincent, who cares for my property in Bedford. Again, I am always concerned with price but NOT more than value. And when the people selling me anything demonstrate that what they are selling is greater than the sum of its parts or more substantial than the standard offering made by lesser providers, I buy on the basis of heart, faith, trust, and respect. Because these are the values they are really selling me and that I am really buying.

As I noted from the outset, I am establishing a metaphor. I know that God is not really a salesman. He has nothing to hawk. He is not out for a profit. But in His way of building trust, faith, love, and assurance, He keeps us tethered to Him with passion and intellect and love. As we go through our various roles of selling as actual salespeople on the job, parents guiding our children, or teachers educating students, the primary lesson we learn from The Master is that if we commit to our customers, clients, and everyone else who means a great deal to us— and if we demonstrate beyond a shadow of doubt that our loyalty is ironclad and bulletproof—the loyalty that we will gain in return will be rock hard and enduring. And there will never be a need to hold a sale or to discount anything.

XV

God Always Controls
the Agenda

Walk into a house of worship and you are struck by the presence of a force infinitely greater than you. A force that has written the rules of conduct for all who are within those walls and has complete control over you and the environment you are in. How this force works, and how it manifests its influence is unclear, but its power is evident and undeniable.

A skilled salesman understands this power. I think of it as *controlling the agenda*, and urge you to view it as one of the most powerful sales principles you can study, absorb, and apply. Put simply, it means you do more than attend a critical meeting—anyone can do that. You own it. You control the flow of events. This is vitally important if you are to achieve your goals.

I use this approach in every single selling situation I

engage in. I have used its powers to make sales worth thousands and even millions of dollars. I prepare to control the agenda the way an athlete prepares for game day:

1. Before I enter the arena—be it a prospect's office, boardroom, or factory floor—I plan precisely what I will say and do to command attention. To be the center of attention. The lightning rod. The rule maker. Does this seem presumptuous? Allow me to share with you what I pass on to the people I mentor in my company: "In every meeting between two or more people, someone controls the agenda. The only choice you face is whether it will be you or them. If you are undecided, think of people who attend a meeting and basically audit the session. They say little and contribute even less. In contrast are the lightning rods who dominate the agenda, guide the discussion, and bend the will of the group in their direction. Which do you want to be: a body in a chair or a force for a positive action?"

2. To claim center stage, I say something no one expects. I resist the knee-jerk temptation to engage in small talk. No weather reports or baseball scores are uttered from my lips. That gibberish is fine if you want to bore people to tears: I'm there to make a sale.

At one point, my company was working with former treasury secretary turned leverage buyout king, William Simon. Through my discussions with Simon, I learned that he despised his former colleague Mike Bloomberg, both major domos at Solomon Brothers before Simon went to Washington and Bloomberg created his media company. Being masters of the universe didn't stop Simon and Bloomberg from engaging in a feud as petty as rival siblings fighting over a dead parent's estate. So when I went to see Bloomberg for the first time, I began the meeting with a curve ball out of left field: "I don't believe half the things Bill Simon says about you, Mike."

With those twelve words, I turned the tables on a billionaire who planned to educate me on his business and to control the agenda, but who wound up waiting to hear what I would or would not reveal about the Simon vendetta.

I had him!

3. Lock in visual contact. By throwing your prospects off balance with a surprising comment or statement of facts, you will command center stage. Once you have seized this position, never relinquish it. Do not let the others avoid your eye contact. Once you have the eyes, you have the brain, and if you have the brain, you can make your case and the odds of making the sale rise astronomically.

As you plan your strategy, think of what happens to you the moment you walk into the house of worship. You know instinctively that all power has shifted from you to a greater force. Adapt the principle.

XVI

God Always Preaches to a Flock

oward Hughes once admonished an employee to "stop thinking like an insect."

Great advice. At some point in our careers, we are all guilty of being small-minded. Time to change that forever.

Think of how this applies to a typical selling scenario. A salesperson has obtained a list of prospects who may be interested in purchasing life insurance. They may be newlyweds, first-time parents, or estate planners, but something about their profiles says that they are good bets to buy insurance.

The salesperson acquired the list from a database firm specializing in identifying prospects for insurance agents. List in hand, she hits the phones, calling each prospect one at a time, making her pitch about the importance of life insurance for a family's financial security.

Think of this as a classic by-the-book slow-and-steady approach that is **virtually assured to deny you exceptional success.**

Contrast this with how the great religions recruit and retain followers, believers, and congregants: They gather flocks and preach to them en masse. Can you imagine God sending his word to us one by one from a database? Absolutely not. This reflects a key principle to guide your career: It makes no sense to sell one at a time.

Let's stay focused on the life insurance example. My company has a great deal of experience serving the marketing needs and methodologies of life insurance firms. At one point, the CEO of one of these firms asked me to attend a seminar at New York's Pierre Hotel hosted by a legendary life insurance salesman, Barry Kaye.

As I approached the grand hotel on Manhattan's Fifth Avenue, I was expecting the standard fare seminar: a group of bored people locked in a darkened room half asleep while a wooden speaker talked them through a PowerPoint that had the impact of a handful of Ambien.

To my surprise, I walked into a revival meeting. Hundreds of information-hungry true believers were crammed into an elegant meeting room lit by a chandelier fitting in size and elegance for the Palace of Versailles. At the center of the storm, Kaye is wooing the crowd with an artfully-constructed parable on how to use little-known techniques of financial engineering to build personal wealth. A born showman, Kaye points to compelling images flashed on a video screen, hands out copies of his book *Die Rich and Tax Free*, and fields questions from a flock of waving arms competing for the seer's attention. Within two hours, he will meet, influence, and create relationships with hundreds of prospects, and set more than fifty appointments. What's more, the flock will spread the Kaye gospel virally to friends, family, and business associates as they would seek to share the thrill of discovery at the centerpiece of the Kaye experience.

How would you compare this wave of adoration with the piecemeal process of working your way through a database of prospects one at a time? Not favorably, that's for sure. The question is: How can you develop a flock and preach to it? Consider the following action steps:

- Create a blog that communicates your viewpoints with passion and provocation. For example, one of our clients sells devices designed, in part, to protect the civilian population from chemical attacks launched by terrorists. To broadcast his message, we created a blog which enables the company's CEO, in his role as his firm's chief zealot (read: chief salesman), to reach a massive audience of mothers, fathers, sisters, brothers, teachers, employers, first responders, and civic leaders concerned with and responsible for the safety of others.

Remember, a phone call reaches one person, a successful blog can talk to and influence the world. As The Master demonstrates, your power is magnified exponentially if and when you speak to a flock.

- Host seminars. Much like Barry Kaye, seminars can assemble hundreds or thousands of people to hear your message, and if they like what they hear, to share your thinking and insights with their peers. This puts the power of compounding to work for you.
- Engage in media relations. By offering a compelling idea to the print, broadcast, or Internet press, you may be able to generate news coverage, bringing the product or service that is at the core of your thinking to entire markets overnight. I have done this myself, repeatedly. By issuing a press release, "The Marketing Manifesto"—suggesting how companies can vastly improve the return on investment (ROI) from their marketing budgets (in great part by defying conventional wisdom on the *right* way to

conduct the marketing process), I have made *news* on Fox TV, the *Wall Street Journal*, *Time* magazine, *USA Today*—and a host of media outlets. And all of this drives traffic to my Websites and my blogs.

It all comes down to leveraging the power of numbers. Small thinkers talk to small numbers of people. "Hello, how are you? Want to buy? Yes or no!" And on and on, one-by-one.

Big thinkers spread the gospel to the biggest possible groups, who spread the message virally and reinforce the thinking and the message among themselves. You put a puck on the ice—they take it from there.

Peter Lynch is a perfect example. As the manager of Fidelity's Magellan Fund, Lynch took his personal investment philosophy public through publication of a best-selling book *One Up On Wall Street*. Lynch's concept—invest in companies you are familiar with and passionate about—created a cult of investors who viewed the author and his fund (which would become the biggest in the United States) as a spiritual/financial leader. No way Lynch was going to call prospects. He created a legion of true believers, a congregation, and became wealthy and powerful in the process.

XVII

God Never Deals in Commissions

magine this typical scenario: A salesperson heads out the door to see a prospect, calculating the commissions he will earn as he races to the meeting. Is this old-fashioned drive and ambition—the DNA of the charm-them-and-close-them sales star—or is it something less? Something false, impatient, and plastic that actually places a ceiling on the salesperson's ability to achieve true and enduring success?

Let me ask you to answer the question yourself. Imagine again the salesperson darting out the door with visions of commissions, like Christmas sugar plums before his eyes. What's wrong with this picture? Well, it's really quite simple: He is focused not on how to truly surprise and enthrall his prospects but, instead, on how to profit from them.

Contrast this with another dramatically different

perspective: You turn to God over and over again, seeking His blessings, His strength, and His solace. Do you think He is calculating the commissions? Of course not. And more to the point of this book, your faith would dissipate if that were part of the equation in any way. The dignity and piety of the relationship would be dealt a lethal blow.

As I have noted, none of us are God. And when we are functioning as salespeople, we must earn commissions of one form or another as compensation for our work. And the better the job we do, the more we should earn. The issue I am addressing, and that we can learn so well from The Master, lies in the focus and degree of your behavior as a salesperson. If you put commissions before service, dedication, and commitment, you will be ignoring the ways of The Master. And you will be limiting your potential as a salesperson, as a successful human being, as one who thrives and grows spiritually and financially by being of extraordinary value to your customers.

In the course of an exceptional day I spent with Bill Gates when he was but a promising young man on the rise, I asked him if he thought much about money. Gates didn't look me in the eyes: He controls the agenda with arrogance, impatience, and knife-sharp intellect. From the moment you meet him, you know that you are in the company of an extraordinary figure, making history as he expresses his philosophy and lives it.

Gates' answer to my question was sharp-tongued and unequivocal: "Thinking a lot about money is the best way to make sure you never earn a great deal of it. Far wiser is to focus on a passion, on something powerful you can do to change peoples' lives. I have always believed that the money will then follow."

In lieu of focusing on commissions, exceptional salespeople ask themselves:

- How can I give my clients far more than they expect?
- How can I demonstrate an extraordinary level of commitment?
- How can I anticipate prospects' needs before they ask for them?
- How can I demonstrate a true sense of partnership?

Let's equate this to another misconception and how it can be challenged and reversed to achieve exceptional success. There is a school of thought that portrays toughness as a prerequisite for winning. If you want to succeed in business, this philosophy advises that your have to crush your adversaries. It's all embedded in the "nice guys finish last" ethos that in some circles passes as doctrine.

What nonsense! What an ugly sentiment. And what flawed thinking that can only result in flawed strategy. I'm not saying that strength, confidence, and mental toughness are not important attributes for success. They are. But you can be strong, confident, and tough without being cold, callous, and mean-spirited. In fact, you should be. And I'm not talking about issues of morality. Let's put that aside for a moment. There is a vital but oft-ignored principle at work here: Beginning any transaction by understanding what the other person wants can make you infinitely more successful in convincing them to do what you want. To *sell* them.

When I spent that day with Bill Gates, Microsoft was in the early days of its meteoric trajectory. Although many viewed Gates as just another techno nerd, he was already the next John D. Rockefeller in the making. As we chatted on a bench on Microsoft's campus, employees tossing Frisbees through the air and holding brainstorming sessions on grassy knolls, I asked Gates how someone so young could have already established himself as a superb negotiator, having outsmarted IBM while he was still in his twenties. Rocking back and forth in an unusual childlike fashion (an eccentricity now hidden from the media by his handlers), Gates remained uncharacteristically silent as he pondered the question. And then, as if it struck him for the first time, he answered.

"People who enter negotiations focused exclusively on what they want are determined, in a macho way, to deny the other guy what he wants," Gates said. "I prefer to understand what the other party wants and plan a strategy to see if I can deliver a solution that satisfies their need while fitting that comfortably into my goal. If I can do that, it's not a battle, it's alliance. A collaboration."

The popular view of Gates is that of a ruthless and unyielding businessman. But this perceived determination to vanquish his opponents and to defeat then in Napoleonic style would have never worked in the boardrooms where Gates has always excelled. A tough veneer yes, but a wise and flexible mind for creating one of the world's greatest companies—and its mightiest personal fortune.

Negotiating successfully is just another form of selling. It drives home the point that if you take the time to understand what your prospects and customers really want, you can serve their needs, and yours, simultaneously.

XVIII

God Never Uses a Laptop

You see it all the time. A salesperson creates a presentation extolling his company's products and services and then downloads it into a laptop for portability and easy use with prospects. He arrives at the sales call, initiates painfully boring small talk, and then voila, opens the laptop and asks the prospects to gather around the small screen for the show.

Convenient? Yes. Easy? Yes.

But does it have passion? Does it come alive?

Absolutely not. Just the opposite. The laptop becomes the center of attention (big mistake . . . remember the importance of controlling the agenda). Here's the real hitch: Because it is neat and portable and right at his fingertips, it makes life easier for the salesman in every way but one: in selling.

Let me put this in perspective: I often stroll through

the Renaissance art galleries of New York's Metropolitan Museum of Art. The experience is overwhelming, transporting me back in time and even more so to another dimension. In this environment, without the aid of a single spoken word, I understand with ever-greater clarity, the power of God. Religion influenced the Renaissance artists on the only important subject worthy of their artistry—and the artists reveal the majesty of a greater Being. We see Jesus at birth. We witness His crucifixion. We cry for Mary. Would a laptop presentation on anything do the same? Of course not. That's why great salesmen never rely on crutches. They use their personal magnetism to transport their customers and prospects to another dimension. To see and experience something so powerful that it transcends the products or services at hand.

Let's switch gears for a moment while keeping this principle intact. In the 1950s, soft drink bottlers were hit by law suits claiming customers had swallowed glass that chipped off in the bottles. To many observers, the suits appeared to be open and shut. Empirical evidence pointed to a flaw in the bottles, resulting in verdicts that would decimate the companies.

And then to the rescue came an extraordinary lawyer who understood the limitations of scientific documents and so-called expert witnesses. Recognizing instinctively that a great lawyer is a great showman, a salesman, this barrister would stand before the jury in open court, crack open a bottle of soda against a mahogany slab, and then drink from it.

"Ladies and gentlemen of the jury, would I dare drink from this cracked bottle if there were the slightest chance of swallowing glass? The claims you have heard are myths . . . nothing more than would-be extortion."

With that, he would take another hearty drink from the bottle and return to his seat. Point made. Case closed.

XIX

God Is a Magnet

People turn to God for a myriad of reasons. The need for faith. For salvation, inspiration, true meaning in life. But whatever the reason, note that I suggested "People turn to God." This is a powerful differentiator between the way God *sells* and the way the standard-fare salesperson does his business. He knocks on doors. He makes phone calls. He sends letters. He forces his way into the lives of his prospects rather than allowing them to "turn to" him. The question is: Why don't human, mortal salespeople find a way to stand for something, to make a statement, to be perceived as a mind and a voice that brings wisdom as opposed to products and services? To be a force people will want to turn to? The answer is clear: The traditional sales-training pabulum focuses on the granular level—on elevator speeches, calls to action, product specifications, and pricing scenarios. On everything but prompting people to turn to you. I have used this principle myself. I understand its power from personal experience. Based on the books I have written, millions of people have come to perceive me as a contrarian's voice on marketing and management. They don't view me as a salesman (which, in part, I am) but more so as a voice of authority on important issues they struggle with. So every day, on multiple occasions, they turn to me. They show up on my company's Websites and in my personal e-mail with either exhilaration or a cry for help. The important point is that I don't search them out; they find me and my firm.

Are you a magnet? Do you stand for anything or do you let the brand you are selling—Coke, Buick, Smith's Hardware—define you? The time has come to find your voice. To understand the power and the importance of the magnet syndrome. To rise above the traditions of selling, and of your industry, and your peers—and to be a person people turn to. Your customers, prospects, children, spouse, friends . . . all because they know that with you they will gain far more than product or service knowledge. And they will get infinitely more than a good deal. They will see the world through a different kind of prism. And that is always invaluable and profound.

About the Author

MARK STEVENS is the CEO of MSCO, a management and marketing firm whose clients include Starwood, GE, Guardian Life, Intrawest, and Estée Lauder. He has written more than twenty books, including *Business Week* bestseller *Your Marketing Sucks*, and *Your Management Sucks*, in which he delivers business insights with blunt truths and unconventional wisdom. Stevens is an in-demand speaker at organizations ranging from Nike and Oracle to the Culinary Institute of America. He is also a frequent guest commentator in print and television media such as the *New York Times*, *Forbes*, and *Fox News*, where he lends his insights and opinions on a wide variety of topics. His wildly successful blog, "Unconventional Thinking" is in the top one percent—out of seventy-two million—of all published blogs.